Oxford School *Shakespeare*

TWELFTH NIGHT

edited by
Roma Gill, OBE
M.A. *Cantab*., B. Litt. *Oxon*

OXFORD
UNIVERSITY PRESS

OXFORD
UNIVERSITY PRESS

Great Clarendon Street, Oxford OX2 6DP

Oxford University Press is a department of the University of Oxford.
It furthers the University's objective of excellence in research,
scholarship, and education by publishing worldwide in

Oxford New York

Auckland Cape Town Dar es Salaam Hong Kong Karachi
Kuala Lumpur Madrid Melbourne Mexico City Nairobi
New Delhi Shanghai Taipei Toronto

with offices in

Argentina Austria Brazil Chile Czech Republic France Greece
Guatemala Hungary Italy Japan Poland Portugal Singapore
South Korea Switzerland Thailand Turkey Ukraine Vietnam

Oxford is a registered trade mark of Oxford University Press
in the UK and in certain other countries

© Oxford University Press 1986
Revised edition first published 1992
First revised edition published 2001
This second revised edition published 2007
British Library Cataloguing in Publication Data available

ISBN: 978 0 19 832583 3

10 9 8 7 6 5 4 3 2

Typeset by Herb Bowes Graphics, Oxford
Printed in Great Britain by Bell and Bain Ltd, Glasgow

Illustrations by Shirley Tourret

Photographs by Donald Cooper/Photostage.
Cover shows Alexandra Mathie as Olivia and
Rebecca Egan as Viola/Cesario in the
Nottingham Playhouse 1995 production of
Twelfth Night.

For Teresa

Oxford School Shakespeare
edited by Roma Gill

A Midsummer Night's Dream
The Taming of the Shrew
Romeo and Juliet
Othello
As You Like It
Hamlet
Macbeth
King Lear
Julius Caesar
Henry V
The Merchant of Venice
The Winter's Tale
Henry IV Part I
Antony and Cleopatra
Twelfth Night
The Tempest
Much Ado About Nothing
Richard II
Measure for Measure
Coriolanus
Love's Labour's Lost

Contents

Acknowledgements

The publisher would like to thank Penguin Books Ltd for their permission to reproduce the music for *O Mistress Mine* and *When that I was and a little tiny boy,* which appeared in Shakespeare: *Twelfth Night* ed. M. M. Mahood (New Penguin Shakespeare, 1968).

Introduction

About the Play

'Twelfth Night' is a name commonly given to the Christian Feast of the Epiphany, which is celebrated on the sixth of January (twelve days after Christmas Day) and which commemorates the coming of the Magi – the three wise men – to the stable in Bethlehem where Christ was born. They brought with them the gifts of gold, frankincense, and myrrh, which were appropriate for an infant king.

Winter festivals

Almost all societies and cultures find it necessary to have some kind of holiday in the middle of winter. The ancient Romans used to hold an annual 'Saturnalia' for about a week in the middle of December. During this period all forms of public order were suspended: the law courts and schools were closed, trading ceased, no criminals were executed, and riotous merry-making was unrestrained. The medieval church throughout Europe adopted this festival, transferring it to the days immediately following Christmas Day (26, 27, and 28 December); on such an occasion, known as the 'Feast of Fools', the clergy in the cathedral towns would elect a boy chorister to be their 'king' for the day, while they feasted and made mockery of those things that they normally held sacred. In England this celebration ceased with the Reformation in the sixteenth century and its place was taken – so far as Queen Elizabeth and her court were concerned – by the 'Twelfth Night' festivities on 6 January.

An Elizabethan entertainment

The regular programme of events began in the morning when the Queen, accompanied by the entire court and her guests, attended chapel and she made a token offering of the Epiphany gifts. The religious ritual was followed by a sumptuous banquet. Then there was the entertainment.

It has been suggested that Shakespeare's play *Twelfth Night* was intended as such an entertainment,[1] and certainly anyone who has

---

[1] In a very imaginative study by Leslie Hotson, *The First Night of 'Twelfth Night'* (London: 1954)

experienced Christmas television programmes will agree that all the proper amusement for a festive season is to be found in this comedy. It is, above all, *funny*. The humour is not all of the same kind: it ranges from the farce of Sir Andrew's near-duel to the slick word-play of Feste – and it allows maybe a few tears of happiness when Viola's lonely courage is rewarded by the man she loves. There is romance, in the story of Olivia as well as in the success of Viola – and even Maria has her triumph with Sir Toby. There are songs – old and new, sentimental lyrics and riotous drinking-songs. And there is dancing as the two drunken knights imitate the steps of the formal Elizabethan measures.

These elements have no date: they appeal immediately to all ages. But in other aspects *Twelfth Night* is a play of its own time, and although the topical allusions can be explained in an editor's notes, the modern readers – or audiences – cannot hope to recapture the first delight of the Elizabethans when they heard, for instance, that the humourless steward Malvolio, making an unaccustomed effort to smile, was creasing his face 'into more lines than is in the new map with the augmentation of the Indies' (3, 2, 71–2). We cannot share some of their beliefs, such as the ideas that passion was produced in the liver, and that the human body is made up of the four elements, but even the twenty-first century is still interested in astrology and notions that the planets might have some effect on the lives and natures of men ('Were we not born under Taurus?', 1, 3, 121). The play's first audiences (whether or not Her Majesty was among them) must have been persons of exceptional wit and understanding: much of the comedy comes from allusions to an intellectual culture of remarkable complexity.

Malvolio

The problem of Malvolio is also solved – or ceases to be a problem – if the play is viewed in a 'festival' context. The character is cruelly treated by his enemies when they lock him in a dark room and claim that he is insane; but the treatment seems less severe if we see Malvolio as the caricature of an unpopular public figure, Sir William Knollys, the Controller of Her Majesty's Household. The official position of such a man always makes him vulnerable to satire, and it is his official duty to take it in good part.

Leading Characters in the Play

Viola and Sebastian	Twins, separated from each other in a shipwreck, who arrive independently in Illyria. Viola, for self-protection, disguises herself as a boy (calling herself 'Cesario'), and enters the service of Duke Orsino.
Orsino	The Duke of Illyria, who can think of nothing but his love for Olivia.
Olivia	A rich countess, who rejects Orsino's love and appears to be still grieving for her brother's death.
Malvolio	The steward in charge of Olivia's household, who aspires to marry his mistress.
Maria	Olivia's lady-in-waiting who is in love with Sir Toby, and who organizes the plot against Malvolio.
Sir Toby Belch	A relation of Olivia's who has taken up residence with the countess; he disrupts the household with his drunken rioting, and proves a very expensive friend to Sir Andrew.
Sir Andrew Aguecheek	A foolish knight whose name suggests his appearance (shivers and pallor are symptoms of the *ague* = a malarial fever).
Feste	A professional jester who serves Olivia as an official fool, but also moves freely between her house and the Duke's palace. He interprets the characters and seems to comment on the action rather than participating in it.

Synopsis

ACT 3

SCENE 1   Viola/Cesario encounters Feste and the two knights; Olivia declares her love for Orsino's messenger.

SCENE 2   Sir Andrew's suspicions have been aroused and he threatens to go home, but Sir Toby coaxes him to challenge Viola/Cesario to a duel.

SCENE 3   Antonio dare not accompany Sebastian on his sight-seeing tour of Orsino's city, but insists on lending him money.

SCENE 4   Olivia is amazed at Malvolio's strange behaviour, and gives him into the care of Sir Toby, who is busy making sure that the two duellists are both terrified of each other. Antonio rescues Viola, whom he mistakes for Sebastian, but is forced to ask for the return of his money.

ACT 4

SCENE 1   Feste and Sir Toby mistake Sebastian for his twin, but their attempt to renew the fighting is interrupted by Olivia.

SCENE 2   Malvolio is locked in a dark room and treated like a madman, but Sir Toby is ready to put an end to the joke.

SCENE 3   Sebastian is astonished when Olivia demands that he should marry her.

ACT 5

SCENE 1   Antonio is brought before Orsino; Olivia claims Viola/Cesario as her newly-betrothed husband; Sir Toby and Sir Andrew complain about their encounter with Sebastian. The twins are reunited, two marriages are arranged – and Malvolio is released from his prison.

Twelfth Night: Commentary

ACT 1

SCENE 1   In his rich ducal palace the young Orsino seems bored and depressed; he calls for music, but is immediately tired of the tune. Other members of his company try to amuse him – this is, after all, their job. They are not really Orsino's friends but courtiers, attendant lords like Curio, who must address their master with respect as 'my lord', smile at his wit in the word-play on 'hart' and 'heart', and show admiration for the clever way in which he compares himself to Actaeon (the hunter in Greek mythology who was turned into a stag and pursued by his own hounds). Orsino fancies that he is in love with Olivia, and his passion increases when he hears, once again, that she has refused to entertain his messenger.

    The atmosphere of the short scene seems overheated. Orsino talks most, and his tone is languid and meditative. He leaves the stage in search of 'sweet beds of flowers' on which he can lie and indulge his daydreams.

SCENE 2   The next scene brings a breath of fresh salt sea air as the characters – Viola and those who have escaped with her from a shipwreck – speak with urgency: they have just escaped death by drowning, and must now make plans for their survival. Viola's first thought is for her brother; he is still missing but Viola refuses to believe that he is dead. The Captain tries to encourage her hope, and helps her to plot her immediate future in this foreign country. She makes a vigorous start towards a new life: 'Lead me on'.

SCENE 3   The first two scenes contrasted, through the movement of the verse, the ineffectual languor of Orsino's court and the realistic energy with which Viola reacts to the loneliness of her new situation. A change to prose in the third scene heralds comedy, as Sir Toby Belch discusses with Maria the accomplishments of his friend, Sir Andrew Aguecheek, who is being presented as a suitor for Olivia. Maria has a sharp answer to every one of Sir Toby's remarks in praise of his friend, and when Sir Andrew appears on the scene we are prepared to find 'a very fool and a prodigal'. Sir Andrew does not disappoint our expectations, making a clumsy attempt – prompted by Sir Toby – to flirt with Maria. He is himself, however, dissatisfied with Olivia's rejection of him, and threatens to leave Illyria – to the dismay of Sir Toby who has been drinking at the thin knight's expense and cannot afford to lose him now! With gross flattery, he persuades Sir Andrew that Olivia must love him for his accomplishments; and the scene ends as the two knights caper around the stage in a parody of all the most elegant Elizabethan dances.

These first three scenes have introduced us to the three main situations in the play: to the love-sick depression of Orsino in his ducal palace; to the loneliness of Viola, cast ashore on a foreign coast; and to the jollity of Olivia's house (although this is not shared by its owner, who has yet to enter the play). After these introductions, the action of the play is ready to begin.

SCENE 4   Disguised as a boy, and calling herself Cesario, Viola has won the trust and respect of a new master, Orsino, who has confided in her all the secrets of his love for Olivia. Now Viola is to be the go-between – but there is a major complication. Viola finds that there is a terrible conflict between her duty to her master and her own desires: she is sent to court Olivia on Orsino's behalf: 'a barful strife! Whoe'er I woo, myself would be his wife'.

SCENE 5   Again, the change to prose signals a more relaxed attitude, although the wit is now intellectual, demanding quicker responses from the audience than the early comic capers of Sir Toby and Sir Andrew. Maria is trying to force a confession from Feste, but she is no match for the professional jester. Feste next proceeds to demonstrate his skill before Olivia, using the syllogistic arguments beloved of Elizabethan scholars. With a daring parody of the catechism of the Church of England, he proves that it is his mistress, and not himself, who is the real fool – but his wit does not amuse Malvolio who, as Olivia's steward, is responsible for the proper conduct of her household. He holds a position of importance, and one which inevitably creates enemies among those who must be disciplined, but even Olivia finds that the steward is somewhat too strict, over-reacting to any supposed affront to his dignity: 'O you are sick of self-love, Malvolio, and taste with a distempered appetite'. When Malvolio has left the stage, however, she warns Feste that some people dislike his fooling – but he seems to place himself under her protection, and helps her to handle the drunken Sir Toby.

Malvolio returns to the stage to describe, with disdain, the persistence of the latest ambassador from Orsino. Intrigued by such determination, Olivia agrees to see him – but hides her identity behind a veil.

Viola/Cesario starts the wooing with a most elegant speech – but after only the first line her common sense asserts itself and she insists upon knowing the identity of her listeners, being reluctant to 'cast away' on a servant the speech that she has so carefully composed and taken so much trouble to learn by heart. Having resisted Maria's attempt to get rid of her, Viola succeeds in dismissing both Maria and all the attendants, so that she is left alone with Olivia. The veil is drawn, and Viola sees Olivia's beauty. She can find no trace of cosmetic painting – which the Elizabethans abhorred – and her praise is simple and sincere:

> 'Tis beauty truly blent, whose red and white
> Nature's own sweet and cunning hand laid on.

Olivia is surprised, but retaliates with a spirited fancifulness and pretends that her beauty is to be sold at an auction. When Viola describes how *she* would demonstrate her love, it is clear that Olivia is much attracted to Orsino's messenger, and Viola's scorn when she is offered payment makes her still more attractive. The device of the ring declares Olivia's passion even more plainly than her confused words at the end of the scene.

ACT 2

SCENE 1   Just as the plot begins to get tangled, Shakespeare gives us an indication that all will end happily: Sebastian is alive, and in Illyria, and he will save the situation. This very careful prose scene makes us sure of his identity – and throughout the rest of the play we can laugh with confidence at the problems of the other characters because we know that there will be a happy resolution for them.

Sebastian has found a true friend in Antonio, the sea-captain who rescued him from the shipwreck. Although he is a minor figure in the play, Antonio is a much-valued character for the unselfish generosity and humility with which he follows the fortunes of his young master.

SCENE 2   Quite unlike the sea-captain is Malvolio, Olivia's steward, who shows his high self-esteem and arrogance in the contempt with which he tries to give his mistress's ring to Viola. After he has flounced off the stage, Viola meditates on the meaning of the ring; she interprets correctly, and neatly summarizes the confusions caused by her disguise:

As I am man,
My state is desperate for my master's love:
As I am woman (now, alas the day!)
What thriftless sighs shall poor Olivia breathe?

Any momentary pathos evoked by this predicament is immediately forgotten in the noisy laughter of the next scene.

SCENE 3   Sir Toby and Sir Andrew have been drinking, and although it is well after midnight they persuade Feste to sing for them and then all join in a noisy chorus, ignoring Maria's warnings. They even scoff at Malvolio, who has been sent by Olivia to silence their riotous behaviour and who, when they will not obey, returns to his mistress to report on their contempt for her orders. The guilty merrymakers (perhaps a little afraid and subdued at Malvolio's words) plan to make a fool of the steward in revenge for his scolding. Sir Toby asks Sir Andrew for more money, and the knights go off for another drink, having decided that it is 'too late to go to bed now'.

SCENE 4   The action sobers again in this scene as Orsino bids 'good morrow, friends' and calls for *his* kind of music; Feste again will be the singer when the raucous drinking-songs change to tender love-lyrics. Before he arrives from Olivia's house, Orsino and Viola begin their debate on the nature of love which is the central subject of this scene. Orsino speaks for all romantic lovers: Viola is a realist. She takes this opportunity, however, of declaring her love for the duke; the audience understands the real meaning of her words, although Orsino (who believes himself to be addressing his page, Cesario) is deceived by the references to the page's 'sister' whose history is 'a blank' and who 'never told her love'. In this scene the actress who plays the part of Viola sometimes presents the character as though she were asking for our sympathy – pity for the plight of a lonely orphan, with no protective brother or friends, hopelessly in love with a man to whom she cannot reveal her secret passion. But this is not Viola as I understand the character. I see a resolute young woman, who faces the difficulties of her situation with energy and wit, refusing to be a victim of circumstances and even determined – from the very beginning of the play – that Orsino is the man who can help her: on first hearing his name (in Scene 2) her reaction suggests a plan:

Orsino! I have heard my father name him:
He was a bachelor then.

Viola is a complex character; like all Shakespeare's best creations, she is a mixture of different, even contradictory, qualities – just like most real human beings!

As soon as it has aroused Orsino's interest, the pathetic little story of Cesario's 'sister' ends – with a riddle which is plain enough to the spectators of the play but puzzling to Orsino; and even Viola/Cesario does not know the full meaning of her words:

> I am all the daughters of my father's house,
> And all the brothers too; and yet I know not . . .

When Viola speaks of love she does not use the extravagant language that characterizes Orsino's passion: her words are simple, direct and sincere. We could almost forget – for the moment – that we are watching a play.

SCENE 5   Now the action changes into a comedy which is highly *theatrical*, where we are expected to believe that we are in Olivia's garden and that the two knights (with their friend Fabian) are hidden in the thick bush of a box-tree. Yet though they are concealed from Malvolio's view, their words and actions are evident to us, the audience, who must remember that Sir Andrew himself has aspirations to win Olivia's hand, and that Malvolio (despite his proud self-righteousness) is merely Olivia's steward – not her social equal.

The comedy starts with Malvolio day-dreaming – and the comments of the onlookers. It is not love for Olivia that motivates his actions, but the ambition 'To be Count Malvolio' and show disdain for 'my kinsman Toby'. These characteristics are demonstrated *before* Malvolio finds the forged letter – preparing the audience for his attempts to decipher its message to suit his own wishes. Maria's trick succeeds; and when she returns at the end of the scene it is to lead us all – the audience as well as the spectators behind the box-hedge – on to the next episode in which Malvolio will appear before Olivia

> in yellow stockings, and 'tis a colour she abhors; and cross-gartered, a fashion she detests; and he will smile upon her, which will now be so unsuitable to her disposition . . .

ACT 3

SCENE 1   Now Shakespeare begins to interweave his different plots, introducing Viola/Cesario to the two knights. She is already familiar with Feste, whom she encountered briefly at Orsino's court. Here she speaks directly to the jester, showing a wit that is almost a match for his professional talents. This is a new aspect of Viola's character: the shipwrecked 'damsel in distress' could not have joked in this light-hearted manner, and it would have been inappropriate – even impertinent – for 'Cesario' to talk like this in Orsino's presence. Feste cleverly begs for money, which is readily given because it has been earned by the fool's talent. Viola's words, when she is alone, show her respect for the professional skill of the clown and for the 'folly which he wisely shows' – which is quite different from the stupidity of some apparently 'wise men' – that is, those who claim to be sensible and who would scorn a fool.

Such a man now appears in the guise of Sir Andrew, who attempts to create a good impression with his French greeting. He seems to be disconcerted by Viola's quick retort (probably spoken with a better French accent than his own), and his admiration increases when the Duke's page addresses Olivia in words that Sir Andrew could never have produced. It is only a brief encounter – just long enough for Sir Andrew to realize that he now has a rival for Olivia's affections.

The more serious business of the scene follows when Olivia is left alone with the person whom she knows as 'Cesario' and to whom she now declares her love. The situation is embarrassing for both characters – for Olivia, because she must speak of love to a 'man' who is socially inferior to her, and for Viola, because she must hear these sentiments and react to them as though she were indeed a man. She manages to handle the interview with an elegant dignity, always remaining loyal to her master, Orsino, and speaking frankly to Olivia ('you do think you are not what you are'). She hints at a mystery ('I am not what I am'), and departs with grace and sincerity in her voice ('By innocence I swear, and by my youth').

SCENE 2   It appears, however, that there has been a witness to this scene who, although he could not hear what was spoken, has taken great offence at what he has seen: 'I saw your niece do more favours to the Count's servingman than ever she bestowed upon me'. Sir Toby flatters Sir Andrew with a new interpretation of the episode, provoking him to fight the duke's page (or, at least, to challenge Cesario to a duel). The scene is written in a fast-moving prose, packed so densely with jests that a contemporary audience would not have had time to breathe between the laughs. Then Maria calls us all to laugh ourselves into stitches at the sight of Malvolio, fooled by the letter into the costume and conduct that were recommended to him.

SCENE 3   But just before the comedy proceeds, Shakespeare inserts another reassuring scene with Sebastian. The verse is simple and straightforward as Antonio explains why he cannot accompany Sebastian on his sight-seeing tour of the city. The short scene provides a little interval – a rest in the laughter – before the comedy reaches its height with the complications of misunderstanding and mistaken identity.

SCENE 4   Olivia speaks first, in words that are not intended to be overheard, wondering how to receive Cesario. She sends for Malvolio and hears from Maria that the steward is acting very strangely and may even be 'possessed' by the devil – in other words, completely and dangerously mad. Malvolio's appearance confirms this report: he is strangely dressed and speaks to his mistress with leering hints quite foreign to his usual formal manners. When he is briefly alone, Malvolio's soliloquy shows the extent to which he flatters himself. Sir Toby approaches, picking up Maria's suggestion that Malvolio is insane and speaking as if to a child. After Malvolio leaves the stage, the three conspirators (Fabian has accompanied Sir Toby) comment on the success of their device with the observation that

> If this were played upon a stage now, I would condemn it as an improbable fiction.

This remark perhaps prevents the theatre audience from voicing the same idea!

The treatment – or punishment – that is now planned for Malvolio is the usual Elizabethan prescription for madness; Malvolio is to be kept in darkness and bound until the devil leaves him. Another form of insanity – 'More matter for a May morning' – is introduced when Sir Andrew brings the letter of challenge. Shakespeare now returns to Viola, marking the transition with a change from prose to verse which allows for a momentary seriousness as Olivia declares her love. Another comic misunderstanding follows (with a return to prose) when Sir Toby delivers his friend's challenge to Viola; and the comedy is re-doubled when he returns to Sir Andrew. But the duel is stopped before it has started by the sudden and unexpected intervention of Antonio. This is a brilliant theatrical stroke, all the more effective because, on looking back at the play, we can see that Shakespeare has in fact prepared us for this moment, first by introducing Antonio as the friend of Sebastian (Viola's identical twin), and then by showing us how and why the two friends have separated from each other.

But the next episode is a sorrowful one for Antonio, when he is arrested at Sir Toby's command – and we must remember that he told Sebastian that Illyria is a dangerous town for him: 'if I be lapsed in this place, I shall pay dear' (3, 3, 36–7). Even though we understand the mistake, we must feel great sympathy for him when Viola cannot return his purse: Antonio is risking his life to help the boy – Sebastian – whom he loves; and it now appears that he is rejected and refused in his moment of need:

> But Oh how vile an idol proves this god!
> Thou hast, Sebastian, done good feature shame.

His mention of her brother's name raises Viola's hopes at once, and we can see that her problems will soon be solved. But there are still more mistakes to come – and also more comedy.

ACT 4

SCENE 1   Sebastian is now drawn into one of the play's major plots; he encounters Feste – and is, of course, mistaken for Viola/Cesario, who is completely identical in dress and appearance. But the twins *are* clearly distinguished from each other by their manner of speech: when Viola jested with Feste in Act 3, Scene 1 she spoke to the fool with a witty sophistication that almost equalled his own, whereas Sebastian, in the present scene, shows impatience with Feste's fooling. The same impatience characterizes his reactions to Sir Andrew and Sir Toby – who also mistake him for 'Cesario'. Finally Olivia receives Sebastian as though he were the one she loves, speaking her sincerity in verse. And Sebastian, enchanted, responds to her: 'If it be thus to dream, still let me sleep'.

SCENE 2   The next scene is not a dream but a nightmare! Most comedy involves pain of some kind: the spectators laugh, but the person who is the object of the laughter may not share the enjoyment. Here Maria and Sir Toby take pleasure in duping Malvolio, and Feste has a double delight, both exercising his acting skill *and* taking revenge on Malvolio. But we begin to feel sorry for the steward, tormented so expertly by his enemies and powerless to help himself. The clowning is brilliant – but it begins to hurt. Already Sir Toby is beginning to feel uneasy: 'I would we were well rid of this knavery'. When Feste sheds his disguise and taunts Malvolio in his own voice, the steward pleads with the fool, but there is still some dignity in his request – and it seems as though Feste will not stop the torture until all Malvolio's pride is gone and he begs for Feste's help, promising to 'requite it in the highest degree'.

SCENE 3   As Feste sings himself off the stage, a bewildered Sebastian appears, musing at his sudden good fortune. There is nevertheless a sense of urgency in the verse, especially when he is joined by Olivia who intends that they should marry at once.

ACT 5

SCENE 1   After a light-hearted battle of wits between Orsino and Feste (in which Feste cleverly begs two coins from the Duke) the comedy seems to be threatened with seriousness. Antonio was speaking the truth when, separating from Sebastian in Act 3, Scene 2, he told the boy that he would 'pay dear' if he should be arrested in Illyria. Orsino is stern – although even in his censure of Antonio he acknowledges the 'fame and honour' of the captain.

But confusions, complications, and explanations follow fast upon each other: Viola is claimed as Sebastian, his friend, by Antonio and as Cesario, her newly-wed husband, by Olivia; she is threatened as a rival by both Orsino and Sir Andrew; and she is finally recognized as herself by her brother. The changing moods of the scene are most strongly marked by the changes from verse to prose; and the pace varies from the speed with which Sir Toby and Sir Andrew are dismissed to the slow caution of the verse that reveals the identities of the shipwrecked twins. Olivia claims her husband, and Orsino looks to find a wife in his former page, reminding Viola that, as Cesario, she had said 'a thousand times Thou never shouldst love woman like to me'. Verse again gives way to prose when Malvolio is remembered and the facts about his 'madness' are revealed by Feste and Fabian. The comedy ends with a dignified verse speech from the ill-used steward, in which he declares his presumptuous ambitions as well as his injuries, and is itself enough to answer his question: 'Tell me why?'. But Malvolio has not learned the lesson that the deception was intended to teach him, and he leaves the stage in a bad temper, determined on revenge. He alone is excluded from the general happiness which unites the other characters.

The play ends with a song from Feste which insists on 'the wind and the rain' of everyday life, directing the audience away from the crazy, enchanted realm of Illyria because now 'our play is done'. It is time for applause.

Source, Text, and Date

The immediate source for Shakespeare's play is a prose narrative, 'The Tale of Apolonius and Silla', which was told by Barnabe Riche in *Riche his Farewell to Militarie Profession* (1581). Riche tells how Silla loved Duke Apolonius, 'a very young man' whom she had met at her father's house in Cyprus. He was a soldier, however, and took no notice of the girl's attentions. Eventually he returned to his home in Constantinople. Silla followed him, but her ship was wrecked in a storm. She managed to save herself by clinging to a sea-chest, and on reaching land she disguised herself as a boy (in clothes that she found in the same chest) and went to Duke Apolonius. She offered to serve him as a page, calling herself by the name of her own brother, 'Silvio'.

'"Silvio" pleased his master so well, that above all the rest of his servants about him, he had the greatest credit, and the Duke put him most in trust' (see Act 1, Scene 4, 1–14).

Apolonius sent his page with love-messages to a widow, Julina, but she rejected the Duke's appeals – and instead fell in love with 'Silvio'. One day, however, the *real* Silvio came to Constantinople in search of his sister, Silla. Julina (mistaking him for the Duke's page) invited him into her house. They made love, and Julina became pregnant; but the next day Silvio left the city. Apolonius proposed marriage to Julina, but she told him of another man, 'whose wife I now remain by faithful vow and promise'. When her pregnancy became apparent, Julina named 'Silvio' as the father of her child. Apolonius threatened to kill his page, but Silla revealed herself to Julina, telling how she had left her father's house and sailed across the sea because of her love for Apolonius. On hearing this, the Duke married Silla – and as soon as her brother learned what had happened, he came back to Constantinople and wedded Julina.

This story did not originate with Barnabe Riche. He found it, in a slightly different form, in a collection of tales[1] by a French writer, Belleforest; and Belleforest made his version from the story told by an Italian writer, Bandello[2]. The ultimate source for these narratives is an anonymous Italian play, *Gl'Ingannati* (*The Deceived Ones*), which was performed in 1531 and published at Venice in 1537.

---

[1] *Histoires Tragiques*, Part IV, No. 59 (1570).
[2] *Novelle*, Part II, No. 36 (1554).

Twelfth Night must have been written at some time between 1599 and 1602. Evidence for the earlier date comes from a topical allusion in Act 3, Scene 2, where Malvolio's smiling face is said to be creased into 'more lines than is in the new map with the augmentation of the Indies' (lines 71–2). The new map in question was first published in 1599. Another clue might be provided by the name Orsino: Don Virginio Orsino, Duke of Bracciano, was a visitor at the court of Queen Elizabeth in the winter of 1600–1. And in 1602 a performance, unlikely to have been the first, was witnessed by John Manningham at a feast in the Middle Temple, and recorded in his *Diary*.

Manningham also recounts an anecdote concerning Queen Elizabeth and one of her relatives, Dr Bullein, which throws light on Fabian's cryptic comment, 'This is to give a dog, and in recompense desire my dog again' (Act 5, Scene 1, 5–6). Dr Bullein was very fond of his dog, and the Queen requested him to grant her one desire – promising to give him in return whatever it was that he wanted. When Queen Elizabeth demanded the dog, Dr Bullein gave it to her; and asked Her Majesty to fulfil her part of the bargain. 'I will,' agreed the Queen. 'Then I pray you, give me my dog again.'

For the present edition I have used the text established in 1975 for the Arden Shakespeare by J. M. Lothian and T. W. Craik.

Shakespeare's Verse

Blank verse

Shakespeare's plays are mainly written in 'blank verse', the form preferred by most dramatists in the sixteenth and early seventeenth centuries. Blank verse has a regular rhythm, but does not rhyme. It is a very flexible medium, which is capable – like the human speaking voice – of a wide range of tones. Easily the best way to understand and appreciate Shakespeare's verse is to read it aloud – and don't worry if you don't understand everything! Try not to be influenced by the dominant rhythm. Instead, decide which are the most important words in each line and use the regular metre to drive them forward to the listeners. Shakespeare used a particular form of blank verse called iambic pentameter.

Iambic pentameter

In iambic pentameter the lines are ten syllables long. Each line is divided into pairs of syllables, or 'feet'. Each 'foot' has one stressed and one unstressed syllable – a pattern that often appears in normal English speech. Here is an example:

> **Orsino**
> If músic bé the foód of lóve, play ón,
> Give mé excéss of ít, that, súrfeitíng,
> The áppetíte may sícken, ánd so díe.
> That stráin agáin, it hád a dýing fáll;
> O, ít came o'ér my éar like thé sweet soúnd
> That bréathes upón a bánk of víoléts,
> Stéaling and gíving ódour. Enóugh, no móre;
> 'Tis nót so sweét now ás it wás befóre.
> O spírit of lóve, how quíck and frésh art thóu,
> That nótwithstánding thý capácitý,
> Recéiveth ás the séa, nought énters thére,
> Of whát valíditý and pítch soé'er,
> But fálls intó abátement ánd low príce
> Evén in á minúte! So fúll of shápes is fáncy,
> That ít alóne is hígh fantásticál.
> **Curio**
> Will yóu go húnt, my lórd?

Orsino

                        What, Cúrio?

Curio

The hárt.

Orsino

Why só I dó, the nóblest thát I háve.   (1, 1, 1–18)

Here the pentameter accommodates a variety of speech tones – the careful regularity of the first lines emphasizes Orsino's self-conscious pose as the romantic lover, delivering beautifully prepared thoughts. His lyrical ecstasy swoons over the 'bank of violets'; it is dismissed with the abrupt 'Enough, no more'; and then it develops into a highly philosophical meditation about the nature of love. Curio's suggestion, 'Will you go hunt, my lord?', brings a note of commonsense – perhaps even of exasperation! Orsino is quick to respond, sharing in the same pentameter as Curio.

In this quotation, the lines are mainly regular in length and normal in iambic stress pattern. Sometimes Shakespeare deviates from the norm, writing lines that are longer or shorter than ten syllables, and varying the stress patterns for unusual emphasis ('Stéaling and gíving ódour. Enoúgh, no móre'). The verse line sometimes contains the grammatical unit of meaning – ''Tis nót so swéet now ás it wás befóre' – thus allowing for a pause at the end of the line, before a new idea is started; at other times, the sense runs on from one line to the next – 'thý capácitý Recéiveth ás the séa'. This makes for the natural fluidity of speech, avoiding monotony but still maintaining the iambic rhythm.

TWELFTH NIGHT

Characters in the Play

Viola (*later disguised as* Cesario) ⎫
Sebastian ⎭ *twins shipwrecked on the coast of Illyria*

Captain *Viola's rescuer in the shipwreck*
Antonio *Sebastian's friend, also a sea-captain*

Orsino *Duke of Illyria*
Valentine ⎫
Curio ⎭ *Gentlemen attending on the* Duke

Olivia *a countess living in Illyria*
Maria *Olivia's lady-in-waiting*
Feste *Olivia's fool*
Malvolio *steward of* Olivia's *household*
Fabian *a member of* Olivia's *household*

Sir Toby Belch *Olivia's uncle*
Sir Andrew Aguecheek Sir Toby's *friend*

A Servant
A Priest

Sailors, Attendants, Musicians, Officers

Scene: Illyria. The action moves between Orsino's court and Olivia's house

ACT 1

Act 1 Scene 1
Orsino, Duke of Illyria, mourns because
Olivia refuses his love.

Os.d. *Illyria*: a country on the eastern
coast of the Adriatic.

3 *appetite*: love's desire for music.
4 *fall*: cadence.
5 *sweet sound*: the sound of a gentle
breeze.

9 *quick and fresh*: keen and hungry.
10–11 *notwithstanding . . . sea*: although
love's desire can hold as much as the
sea.
12 *validity*: value.
pitch: excellence.
13 *falls . . . price*: is cheapened and
loses its value.
14 *shapes*: imaginations.
fancy: love.
15 *it . . . fantastical*: there is nothing that
is more imaginative.

17 *hart*: deer; Orsino, of course, makes a
pun with 'heart'.

20 *purg'd . . . pestilence*: purified the air
(there were frequent epidemics of
infectious plague—'pestilence'—in
the sixteenth century).
21–3 *was I . . . me*: Orsino compares
himself with the hunter Actaeon (in
classical mythology) who was changed
into a stag by the goddess Diana, then
chased and killed by his own hounds.
22 *fell*: savage.

SCENE 1

The Duke's *palace. Music. Enter* Orsino, *Duke of
Illyria,* Curio, *and* Attendants

Orsino
If music be the food of love, play on,
Give me excess of it, that, surfeiting,
The appetite may sicken, and so die.
That strain again, it had a dying fall:
5 O, it came o'er my ear like the sweet sound
That breathes upon a bank of violets,
Stealing and giving odour. Enough, no more;
'Tis not so sweet now as it was before.
O spirit of love, how quick and fresh art thou,
10 That notwithstanding thy capacity
Receiveth as the sea, nought enters there,
Of what validity and pitch soe'er,
But falls into abatement and low price
Even in a minute! So full of shapes is fancy,
15 That it alone is high fantastical.
Curio
Will you go hunt, my lord?
Orsino
                                        What, Curio?
Curio
The hart.
Orsino
Why so I do, the noblest that I have.
O, when mine eyes did see Olivia first,
20 Methought she purg'd the air of pestilence;
That instant was I turn'd into a hart,
And my desires, like fell and cruel hounds,
E'er since pursue me.

Enter Valentine

How now? What news from her?

Valentine
So please my lord, I might not be admitted,
25 But from her handmaid do return this answer:
The element itself, till seven years' heat,
Shall not behold her face at ample view;
But like a cloistress she will veiled walk,
And water once a day her chamber round
30 With eye-offending brine: all this to season
A brother's dead love, which she would keep fresh
And lasting, in her sad remembrance.
Orsino
O, she that hath a heart of that fine frame
To pay this debt of love but to a brother,
35 How will she love, when the rich golden shaft
Hath kill'd the flock of all affections else
That live in her; when liver, brain, and heart,
These sovereign thrones, are all supplied, and fill'd
Her sweet perfections with one self king!
40 Away before me to sweet beds of flowers!
Love-thoughts lie rich when canopied with bowers.
                                    [*Exeunt*

Scene 2

The sea coast: enter Viola, *a* Captain, *and* Sailors

Viola
What country, friends, is this?
Captain
This is Illyria, lady.
Viola
And what should I do in Illyria?
My brother he is in Elysium.
5 Perchance he is not drown'd: what think you, sailors?
Captain
It is perchance that you yourself were sav'd.

---

24 *So . . . lord*: I'm sorry to say, my lord.
26 *element*: sky.
    till . . . heat: until the heat of seven summers is over.
27 *at ample view*: in full sight (i.e. without a veil).
28 *cloistress*: nun (in an enclosed order).
    veiled: veilèd.
30 *eye-offending brine*: salt tears that sting the eyes.
    season: keep fresh (as brine is used to preserve meat and vegetables).
32 *remembrance*: The word must be pronounced with four syllables ('rememberance').
33 *that fine frame*: so sensitively formed.
34 *but*: merely.
35 *shaft*: arrow; Cupid (the god of love) had two kinds of arrow: the one with the golden tip caused love, whilst the leaden arrow brought hatred.
36 *all affections else*: all other emotions.
37-9 *when . . . king*: when those parts of her body that govern the emotions are all dominated by a single ruler.
40-1 *Away . . . bowers*: Orsino's couplet sets a final emphasis on his romantic posturing.

Act 1 Scene 2
Viola has been saved from a shipwreck, but it seems that her twin brother is lost; she decides to seek service in Illyria, disguised as a boy.

4 *Elysium*: heaven, the home of the blessed (in Greek mythology); Viola's grief, unlike Orsino's melancholy, is expressed with brevity and wit.
5 *Perchance*: perhaps; *and also* 'by good fortune'—as in line 6.

'O my poor brother!' (*1*, 2, 7) Harriet Walter as Viola, Royal Shakespeare Company, 1988.

8 *chance*: possibility.
9 *Assure yourself*: be assured.
10 *poor number*: few.
11 *driving*: drifting.
13 *the practice*: what to do.
14 *liv'd*: floated.
15 *Arion*: a Greek musician who threw himself into the sea to escape from murderous sailors and was carried to safety on the back of a dolphin.
16 *hold acquaintance*: maintain friendly contact (i.e. without sinking).
19–21 *Mine . . . him*: my own escape encourages me to hope the same for him, and your words give sanction for this.

Viola
O my poor brother! and so perchance may he be.
   Captain
True, madam, and to comfort you with chance,
Assure yourself, after our ship did split,
10 When you and those poor number sav'd with you
Hung on our driving boat, I saw your brother,
Most provident in peril, bind himself
(Courage and hope both teaching him the practice)
To a strong mast that liv'd upon the sea;
15 Where, like Arion on the dolphin's back,
I saw him hold acquaintance with the waves
So long as I could see.
   Viola
For saying so, there's gold:
Mine own escape unfoldeth to my hope,

20 Whereto thy speech serves for authority,
    The like of him. Know'st thou this country?
        Captain
    Ay, madam, well, for I was bred and born
    Not three hours' travel from this very place.
        Viola
    Who governs here?
        Captain
25 A noble duke, in nature as in name.
        Viola
    What is his name?
        Captain
    Orsino.
        Viola
    Orsino! I have heard my father name him.
    He was a bachelor then.
        Captain
30 And so is now, or was so very late;
    For but a month ago I went from hence,
    And then 'twas fresh in murmur (as, you know,
    What great ones do, the less will prattle of)
    That he did seek the love of fair Olivia.
        Viola
35 What's she?
        Captain
    A virtuous maid, the daughter of a count
    That died some twelvemonth since; then leaving her
    In the protection of his son, her brother,
    Who shortly also died; for whose dear love
40 (They say) she hath abjur'd the company
    And sight of men.
        Viola
                        O that I serv'd that lady,
    And might not be deliver'd to the world,
    Till I had made mine own occasion mellow,
    What my estate is.
        Captain
                        That were hard to compass,
45 Because she will admit no kind of suit,
    No, not the Duke's.

30 *very late*: quite recently.

32 *fresh in murmur*: newly rumoured.
33 *prattle of*: gossip about.

35 *What's she*: what social rank is she.

40 *abjur'd*: renounced.

42–4 *might . . . estate is*: that my position ('estate') might not be made known to the world until the time is ripe.

44 *compass*: arrange.

45 *admit*: take notice of.
    suit: request.

47 *fair behaviour*: honest appearance.
48 *though that*: although.

50 *will*: am prepared to.
51 *character*: appearance.

53 *Conceal*: disguise.
   what I am: my real nature (i.e. as a woman).
54 *haply shall become*: may chance to suit.

57 *worth thy pains*: the Captain himself might benefit.
58 *many sorts*: i.e. instrumental as well as vocal.
59 *allow*: prove.
   worth: suitable for.
60 *hap*: happen.
61 *shape*: adapt.
   wit: invention.
62 *mute*: dumb servant; these, as well as eunuchs, were often employed in positions demanding secrecy.
63 *blabs*: tells tales.
   let . . . see: put out my eyes.

Act 1 Scene 3
Sir Toby, Olivia's kinsman, has taken up residence in her house with his friend, Sir Andrew, who wants to marry Olivia. But their riotous conduct is disturbing the entire household, and Maria advises Sir Toby to mend his ways.

1 *What a plague*: what the devil.
   niece: This (like 'cousin' in line 4) is used loosely to indicate some degree of relationship.
3 *troth*: faith.
4 *takes . . . exceptions*: objects very strongly.
5 *ill hours*: irregular habits.
6 *let . . . excepted*: let her take exception to behaviour which she has already taken exception to; Sir Toby uses a legal phrase (*exceptis excipiendis* = excepting those things which are to be excepted).

Viola
There is a fair behaviour in thee, Captain;
And though that nature with a beauteous wall
Doth oft close in pollution, yet of thee
50 I will believe thou hast a mind that suits
With this thy fair and outward character.
I prithee (and I'll pay thee bounteously)
Conceal me what I am, and be my aid
For such disguise as haply shall become
55 The form of my intent. I'll serve this duke;
Thou shalt present me as an eunuch to him—
It may be worth thy pains—for I can sing,
And speak to him in many sorts of music,
That will allow me very worth his service.
60 What else may hap, to time I will commit;
Only shape thou thy silence to my wit.
   Captain
Be you his eunuch, and your mute I'll be:
When my tongue blabs, then let mine eyes not see.
   Viola
I thank thee. Lead me on.   [*Exeunt*

Scene 3

Olivia's house: enter Sir Toby Belch *and* Maria

Sir Toby
What a plague means my niece to take the death of her brother thus? I am sure care's an enemy to life.
   Maria
By my troth, Sir Toby, you must come in earlier o' nights: your cousin, my lady, takes great exceptions to
5 your ill hours.
   Sir Toby
Why, let her except, before excepted.
   Maria
Ay, but you must confine yourself within the modest limits of order.

9 *confine . . . finer*: a) I will accept no
further restrictions; b) I refuse to
dress more finely. Sir Toby plays with
the sounds and senses of the words.

11 *an'*: if.

11–12 *let them . . . straps*: Sir Toby's
variant of a contemptuous dismissal
phrase, 'hang yourself in your own
garters'.

13 *quaffing*: heavy drinking.
undo: ruin.

18 *tall*: brave; but Maria pretends that Sir
Andrew's height is being described.
as any's: as any man is.

20 *ducats*: Venetian gold coins worth
about 23p.

21 *he'll . . . year*: use up his whole estate
within a year.

22 *very*: true, complete.
prodigal: wastrel.

23 *viol-de-gamboys*: bass-viol.

25 *without book*: by memory.

26 *most natural*: a) quite naturally;
b) like a naturally born idiot.

27–8 *gift of a coward*: talent for
cowardice.

28 *allay*: modify.
gust: enjoyment.

30 *gift of a grave*: be given a grave, get
himself killed.

31 *substractors*: Sir Toby's tipsy coinage
from 'detractors' (= those who
diminish reputation).

33 *add*: Maria plays on Toby's 'subtract'.

Sir Toby

Confine? I'll confine myself no finer than I am. These
10 clothes are good enough to drink in, and so be these
boots too—an' they be not, let them hang themselves in
their own straps.

Maria

That quaffing and drinking will undo you. I heard my
lady talk of it yesterday, and of a foolish knight that you
15 brought in one night here to be her wooer.

Sir Toby

Who, Sir Andrew Aguecheek?

Maria

Aye, he.

Sir Toby

He's as tall a man as any's in Illyria.

Maria

What's that to th' purpose?

Sir Toby

20 Why, he has three thousand ducats a year.

Maria

Ay, but he'll have but a year in all these ducats, he's a
very fool, and a prodigal.

Sir Toby

Fie that you'll say so! He plays o' th' viol-de-gamboys,
and speaks three or four languages word for word
25 without book, and hath all the good gifts of nature.

Maria

He hath indeed all, most natural: for besides that he's a
fool, he's a great quarreller; and but that he hath the gift
of a coward to allay the gust he hath in quarrelling, 'tis
thought among the prudent he would quickly have the
30 gift of a grave.

Sir Toby

By this hand, they are scoundrels and substractors that
say so of him. Who are they?

Maria

They that add, moreover, he's drunk nightly in your
company.

Sir Toby

35 With drinking healths to my niece: I'll drink to her as
long as there is a passage in my throat, and drink in

37 *coistrel*: knave, villain.
38 *turn o'th'toe*: spin round.
   parish top: A large spinning-top, lashed with a whip, provided villagers with exercise and entertainment.
39 *Castiliano vulgo*: keep a straight face (a Castilian countenance); Sir Toby's phrase has never been properly explained.
40 *Agueface*: Sir Toby scoffs at Sir Andrew's appearance ('a thin-faced knave', *5*, 1, 198).

43 *shrew*: little, mouse-like creature (a term usually describing a nagging woman).

45 *Accost*: speak to.

47 *chambermaid*: lady-in-waiting.

51 *front . . . her*: approach her, get aboard her, court her, make an attack on her; Sir Toby's nautical metaphors carry sexual innuendos.
53 *undertake*: tackle.
53–4 *in this company*: in front of all these people; the dramatic illusion is suspended for the momentary comic effect.

56 *An' . . . so*: if you let her leave like this.

Illyria. He's a coward and a coistrel that will not drink to my niece till his brains turn o' th' toe, like a parish top. What, wench! *Castiliano vulgo*: for here comes Sir
40 Andrew Agueface.

Enter Sir Andrew Aguecheek

Sir Andrew
Sir Toby Belch! How now, Sir Toby Belch?
Sir Toby
Sweet Sir Andrew!
Sir Andrew
Bless you, fair shrew.
Maria
And you too, sir.
Sir Toby
45 Accost, Sir Andrew, accost.
Sir Andrew
What's that?
Sir Toby
My niece's chambermaid.
Sir Andrew
Good Mistress Accost, I desire better acquaintance.
Maria
My name is Mary, sir.
Sir Andrew
50 Good Mistress Mary Accost—
Sir Toby
You mistake, knight. 'Accost' is front her, board her, woo her, assail her.
Sir Andrew
By my troth, I would not undertake her in this company. Is that the meaning of 'accost'?
Maria
55 Fare you well, gentlemen.
Sir Toby
An' thou let part so, Sir Andrew, would thou might'st never draw sword again!

59–72 *do you think . . . barren*: The
sexual overtones of this flirtatious
banter need little verbal paraphrase.
59–60 *in hand*: to deal with.
61 *I have . . . hand*: I am not holding
your hand.
62 *Marry*: a mild oath (= by the Virgin
Mary).
63 *thought is free*: the usual retort to the
question 'Do you take me for a fool?'
64 *buttery bar*: ledge made by half-door
of buttery, where drink was served.

65 *What's . . . metaphor*: what do you
mean by talking of a drinking hand.
66 *dry*: a) thirsty; b) impotent (a moist
palm was said to indicate sexual
arousal).
67–8 *I am not . . . dry*: 'Fools have wit
enough to keep themselves out of the
rain' (proverbial).
71 *at . . . ends*: a) have a ready supply of
jokes; b) am holding your hand.
73 *thou lack'st . . . canary*: you need a
drink: 'canary' was a sweet white wine
from the Canary Islands.
74 *put down*: deflated, defeated.
75–6 *put me down*: lay me down (drunk);
rob me of my wits.
76–7 *Methinks . . . has*: sometimes I
think I have no more intelligence than
any ordinary Christian man.
78 *beef*: This was proverbially said to dull
the brains.
79 *No question*: no doubt about it.
80 *forswear*: give it up.
82 *Pourquoi*: why.

Sir Andrew

An' you part so, mistress, I would I might never draw sword again. Fair lady, do you think you have fools in
60 hand?

Maria

Sir, I have not you by th' hand.

Sir Andrew

Marry, but you shall have, and here's my hand.

Maria

Now, sir, thought is free. I pray you bring your hand to th' buttery bar and let it drink.

Sir Andrew

65 Wherefore, sweetheart? What's your metaphor?

Maria

It's dry, sir.

Sir Andrew

Why, I think so: I am not such an ass but I can keep my hand dry. But what's your jest?

Maria

A dry jest, sir.

Sir Andrew

70 Are you full of them?

Maria

Ay, sir, I have them at my fingers' ends: marry, now I let go your hand, I am barren.   [*Exit* Maria

Sir Toby

O knight, thou lack'st a cup of canary: when did I see thee so put down?

Sir Andrew

75 Never in your life, I think, unless you see canary put me down. Methinks sometimes I have no more wit than a Christian or an ordinary man has: but I am a great eater of beef, and I believe that does harm to my wit.

Sir Toby

No question.

Sir Andrew

80 An' I thought that, I'd forswear it. I'll ride home to-morrow, Sir Toby.

Sir Toby

Pourquoi, my dear knight?

84 *tongues*: languages; Sir Toby follows this word with a pun on 'tongs'.
86 *the arts*: education.
88 *mended*: improved.
89 *by nature*: Sir Toby makes a commonplace contrast between nature and art.
90 *becomes me*: suits me.
91 *flax*: a pale yellow fibre (making linen).
   distaff: staff on which flax is wound.

92 *housewife*: The word (pronounced 'hussif') means also 'hussy' (= prostitute)—who might infect Sir Andrew with a venereal disease causing his hair to fall out.
93 *I'll home*: I will go home.
94 *she'll none of me*: she will not be interested in me.
97 *estate*: wealth.
98 *there's life in't*: from the proverb 'While there's life, there's hope.'
100 *masques*: masquerades.

102 *kickshawses*: little trifles (from French *quelquechose*).

103–4 *under . . . betters*: as long as they are not better than I am—i.e. my social superiors.
105 *old*: more experienced.
106 *What is thy excellence*: how good are you.
   galliard: a lively dance with five steps, of which the fifth was a little leap in the air.
107 *cut a caper*: jump about a bit; 'capers' are also little peppery berries served with mutton.
108 *mutton*: a slang term for 'prostitute'.

Sir Andrew
What is '*pourquoi*'? Do, or not do? I would I had bestowed that time in the tongues that I have in fencing,
85 dancing, and bear-baiting. O, had I but followed the arts!

Sir Toby
Then hadst thou had an excellent head of hair.

Sir Andrew
Why, would that have mended my hair?

Sir Toby
Past question, for thou seest it will not curl by nature.

Sir Andrew
90 But it becomes me well enough, does't not?

Sir Toby
Excellent, it hangs like flax on a distaff; and I hope to see a housewife take thee between her legs, and spin it off.

Sir Andrew
Faith, I'll home tomorrow, Sir Toby; your niece will not be seen, or if she be, it's four to one she'll none of me:
95 the Count himself here hard by woos her.

Sir Toby
She'll none o' th' Count; she'll not match above her degree, neither in estate, years, nor wit: I have heard her swear't. Tut, there's life in't, man.

Sir Andrew
I'll stay a month longer. I am a fellow o' th' strangest
100 mind i' th' world: I delight in masques and revels sometimes altogether.

Sir Toby
Art thou good at these kickshawses, knight?

Sir Andrew
As any man in Illyria, whatsoever he be, under the degree of my betters; and yet I will not compare with an
105 old man.

Sir Toby
What is thy excellence in a galliard, knight?

Sir Andrew
Faith, I can cut a caper.

Sir Toby
And I can cut the mutton to't.

109 *back-trick*: backward steps in dancing—with obvious sexual innuendo.

112 *curtain*: Curtains were used to protect pictures from dust and sunlight.
113 *Mistress Mall*: This may be an allusion to Mary Fitton, who was the subject of some court scandal.
114 *coranto*: fast, skipping dance.
115 *jig*: lively, jumping dance.
make water: urinate.
116 *sink-a-pace*: another five-step dance (*cinque pace*)—with a pun on 'sink' = sewer.
117 *virtues*: abilities.
118 *formed . . . galliard*: created (and ordained) by the stars for dancing.
119 *does . . . well*: looks well enough.
119–20 *dun-coloured stock*: dark brown stocking.
121 *Taurus*: the Bull; the signs of the zodiac were believed to govern different areas of the body, but astrologers differed in their assignments.

Sir Andrew
And I think I have the back-trick simply as strong as any
110 man in Illyria.
Sir Toby
Wherefore are these things hid? Wherefore have these gifts a curtain before 'em? Are they like to take dust, like Mistress Mall's picture? Why dost thou not go to church in a galliard, and come home in a coranto? My very walk
115 should be a jig; I would not so much as make water but in a sink-a-pace. What dost thou mean? Is it a world to hide virtues in? I did think, by the excellent constitution of thy leg, it was formed under the star of a galliard.
Sir Andrew
Ay, 'tis strong, and it does indifferent well in a dun-
120 coloured stock. Shall we set about some revels?
Sir Toby
What shall we do else? Were we not born under Taurus?
Sir Andrew
Taurus? That's sides and heart.
Sir Toby
No, sir, it is legs and thighs. Let me see thee caper. Ha, higher! Ha, ha, excellent!   [*Exeunt*

The Zodiac

'On your attendance, my lord, here.'
(*1*, 4, 11) Harriet Walter as Viola/Cesario,
Royal Shakespeare Company, 1988.

Act 1 Scene 4
Viola, disguised as a boy and calling herself
'Cesario', attends on Duke Orsino, and is
sent to Olivia as his ambassador.

3 *but three days*: The play is operating
on more than one time scheme!

5 *humour*: temperament.
negligence: neglect of duty.

SCENE 4

The Duke'*s court: enter* Valentine *and* Viola *dressed
like a man*

Valentine
If the Duke continue these favours towards you,
Cesario, you are like to be much advanced: he hath
known you but three days, and already you are no
stranger.
Viola
5 You either fear his humour, or my negligence, that you
call in question the continuance of his love. Is he
inconstant, sir, in his favours?
Valentine
No, believe me.

Enter Orsino, Curio, *and* Attendants

Viola
I thank you. Here comes the Count.
Orsino
10   Who saw Cesario, ho?
Viola
On your attendance, my lord, here.
Orsino
[*To* Curio *and* Attendants] Stand you awhile aloof.
[*To* Viola] Cesario,
Thou know'st no less but all: I have unclasp'd
To thee the book even of my secret soul.
15   Therefore, good youth, address thy gait unto her,
Be not denied access, stand at her doors,
And tell them, there thy fixed foot shall grow
Till thou have audience.
Viola
                                        Sure, my noble lord,
If she be so abandon'd to her sorrow
20   As it is spoke, she never will admit me.
Orsino
Be clamorous, and leap all civil bounds,
Rather than make unprofited return.
Viola
Say I do speak with her, my lord, what then?
Orsino
O then unfold the passion of my love,
25   Surprise her with discourse of my dear faith;
It shall become thee well to act my woes:
She will attend it better in thy youth,
Than in a nuncio's of more grave aspect.
Viola
I think not so, my lord.
Orsino
                                        Dear lad, believe it—
30   For they shall yet belie thy happy years,
That say thou art a man: Diana's lip
Is not more smooth and rubious; thy small pipe

11 *On your attendance*: at your service.

12 *aloof*: aside.

13 *no . . . all*: absolutely everything.
unclasp'd: unlocked; valuable books were sometimes fitted with locks.

15 *address thy gait*: direct your steps; Orsino's speech suits his affected pose.
16 *access*: The word is stressed on the second syllable.
17 *them*: i.e. the servants at the doors.
fixed: fixèd; firmly planted.
18 *audience*: hearing, attention.
21 *leap . . . bounds*: go beyond the limits of proper behaviour.
22 *make . . . return*: come back empty-handed.
23 *Say I do speak*: suppose I do speak.
24 *unfold*: tell everything about.
25 *Surprise*: suddenly attack and capture (her heart).
26 *become*: suit.
27 *attend it*: listen to it.
28 *nuncio*: messenger.
aspect: appearance (the stress is on the second syllable).
30 *belie*: misrepresent.
31 *Diana*: the virgin goddess of chastity.
32 *rubious*: ruby-red; the word is Shakespeare's coinage.
pipe: piping voice.

33 *organ*: speech organ, voice.
shrill and sound: high-pitched and clear.
34 *semblative*: like (another Shakespearean coinage).
part: a) nature; b) role. Shakespeare alerts the audience to the subtleties of this double disguise—a boy actor playing the part of a girl who disguises herself as a boy.
35 *constellation*: personality (determined at birth by the position of the stars).
right apt: absolutely right.
38 *When . . . company*: i.e. alone.
41 *a barful strife*: a struggle full of obstacles.

Act 1 Scene 5
Feste, the jester, tries to entertain Olivia, but Malvolio, her steward, is not amused. Viola/Cesario encounters Olivia—who immediately falls in love.

2–3 *in way . . . excuse*: to make excuses for you.

5 *colours*: (enemy) flags; Feste also makes a pun with 'collar' (= hangman's noose).
6 *Make . . . good*: prove it.

8 *A . . . answer*: a less than adequate answer; Lent is the season for fasting.

11 *that . . . say*: you can say that with confidence (i.e. that he has been in trouble).
13–14 *God . . . talents*: Feste alludes to the words of the Bible ('unto every one that hath shall be given') and the parable of the talents (St Matthew, chapter 25).
14 *talents*: natural gifts (as opposed to the acquired skills of a professional jester).

Is as the maiden's organ, shrill and sound;
And all is semblative a woman's part.
35 I know thy constellation is right apt
For this affair. Some four or five attend him—
All, if you will: for I myself am best
When least in company. Prosper well in this,
And thou shalt live as freely as thy lord,
40 To call his fortunes thine.
    Viola
                    I'll do my best
To woo your lady. [*Aside*] Yet, a barful strife!
Whoe'er I woo, myself would be his wife.   [*Exeunt*

SCENE 5

Olivia's house: enter Maria *and* Feste

Maria
Nay, either tell me where thou hast been, or I will not open my lips so wide as a bristle may enter, in way of thy excuse. My lady will hang thee for thy absence.
    Feste
Let her hang me: he that is well hanged in this world
5 needs to fear no colours.
    Maria
Make that good.
    Feste
He shall see none to fear.
    Maria
A good lenten answer. I can tell thee where that saying was born, of 'I fear no colours'.
    Feste
10 Where, good Mistress Mary?
    Maria
In the wars, and that may you be bold to say in your foolery.
    Feste
Well, God give them wisdom that have it; and those that are fools, let them use their talents.

Maria

15 Yet you will be hanged for being so long absent; or to be
turned away—is not that as good as a hanging to you?

Feste

Many a good hanging prevents a bad marriage and for
turning away, let summer bear it out.

Maria

You are resolute then?

Feste

20 Not so, neither, but I am resolved on two points.

Maria

That if one break, the other will hold: or if both break,
your gaskins fall.

Feste

Apt, in good faith, very apt. Well, go thy way: if Sir Toby
would leave drinking, thou wert as witty a piece of Eve's

25 flesh as any in Illyria.

Maria

Peace, you rogue, no more o' that. Here comes my lady:
make your excuse wisely, you were best.   [*Exit*

Enter Olivia, *with* Malvolio *and* Attendants

Feste

Wit, an't be thy will, put me into good fooling! Those
wits that think they have thee, do very oft prove fools:

30 and I that am sure I lack thee, may pass for a wise man.
For what says Quinapalus? 'Better a witty fool than a
foolish wit.' God bless thee, lady!

Olivia

Take the fool away.

Feste

Do you not hear, fellows? Take away the lady.

Olivia

35 Go to, y'are a dry fool: I'll no more of you. Besides, you
grow dishonest.

Feste

Two faults, madonna, that drink and good counsel will
amend: for give the dry fool drink, then is the fool not
dry; bid the dishonest man mend himself, if he mend,

40 he is no longer dishonest; if he cannot, let the botcher

44 *syllogism*: argument.
   so: that's all right.
44–5 *what remedy*: what can you do about it.
45–6 *As . . . flower*: Feste's apparently meaningless chatter perhaps suggests that 'calamity' must improve and the flower will fade.

49 *Misprision*: error, misunderstanding.
   in . . . degree: of the very worst kind (a legal term).
49–50 *cucullus . . . monachum*: 'The hood makes not the monk' (proverbial).
51 *motley*: multi-coloured fool's costume.

54 *Dexteriously*: dexterously (= skilfully); an Elizabethan form.

56 *catechize*: ask you some questions (a technique of religious instruction).
56–7 *Good . . . virtue*: my dear, virtuous little creature.
58 *idleness*: amusement.
   bide: wait for.

66 *mend*: improve (in his fooling).

mend him. Anything that's mended is but patched: virtue that transgresses is but patched with sin, and sin that amends is but patched with virtue. If that this simple syllogism will serve, so: if it will not, what
45 remedy? As there is no true cuckold but calamity, so beauty's a flower. The lady bade take away the fool, therefore I say again, take her away.

Olivia
Sir, I bade them take away you.

Feste
Misprision in the highest degree! Lady, *cucullus non*
50 *facit monachum*: that's as much to say, as I wear not motley in my brain. Good madonna, give me leave to prove you a fool.

Olivia
Can you do it?

Feste
Dexteriously, good madonna.

Olivia
55 Make your proof.

Feste
I must catechize you for it, madonna. Good my mouse of virtue, answer me.

Olivia
Well sir, for want of other idleness, I'll bide your proof.

Feste
Good madonna, why mourn'st thou?

Olivia
60 Good fool, for my brother's death.

Feste
I think his soul is in hell, madonna.

Olivia
I know his soul is in heaven, fool.

Feste
The more fool, madonna, to mourn for your brother's soul, being in heaven. Take away the fool, gentlemen.

Olivia
65 What think you of this fool, Malvolio, doth he not mend?

Malvolio
Yes, and shall do, till the pangs of death shake him.

68 *ever*: always.

71–3 *will . . . fool*: will swear freely that I
am not clever (like a fox) but he
couldn't even be bribed to say that
you are not a fool.

75 *barren*: uninspired.
76 *put down*: defeated.
76–7 *an ordinary . . . stone*: A natural
idiot called Stone was a popular
tavern ('ordinary') entertainer.
78 *out of his guard*: defenceless (a
fencing term).
79 *minister occasion*: offer opportunity
(for a joke).
gagged: unable to say anything.
protest: declare.
80 *crow so*: laugh so much.
set kind: professional.
81 *zanies*: stooges, assistants.
83 *distempered*: sick.
83–4 *of free disposition*: good natured.
84 *bird-bolts*: blunt arrows for shooting
birds.
85 *deem*: consider.
86 *allowed*: licensed.
rail: abuse, scold.
89 *Mercury . . . leasing*: may Mercury
(the god of deception) endow you with
the art of lying.

96 *hold him in delay*: are holding him
back.

Infirmity, that decays the wise, doth ever make the
better fool.

Feste

70 God send you, sir, a speedy infirmity, for the better
increasing your folly! Sir Toby will be sworn that I am
no fox, but he will not pass his word for twopence that
you are no fool.

Olivia

How say you to that, Malvolio?

Malvolio

75 I marvel your ladyship takes delight in such a barren
rascal. I saw him put down the other day with an
ordinary fool, that has no more brain than a stone. Look
you now, he's out of his guard already! Unless you laugh
and minister occasion to him, he is gagged. I protest I

80 take these wise men, that crow so at these set kind of
fools, no better than the fools' zanies.

Olivia

O you are sick of self-love, Malvolio, and taste with a
distempered appetite. To be generous, guiltless, and of
free disposition, is to take those things for bird-bolts

85 that you deem cannon-bullets. There is no slander in an
allowed fool, though he do nothing but rail; nor no
railing in a known discreet man, though he do nothing
but reprove.

Feste

Now Mercury endue thee with leasing, for thou speak'st

90 well of fools!

Enter Maria

Maria

Madam, there is at the gate a young gentleman much
desires to speak with you.

Olivia

From the Count Orsino, is it?

Maria

I know not, madam: 'tis a fair young man, and well

95 attended.

Olivia

Who of my people hold him in delay?

Maria

Sir Toby, madam, your kinsman.

Olivia

Fetch him off, I pray you: he speaks nothing but

99 *madman*: like a madman. madman. Fie on him!   [*Exit* Maria

100 *suit*: petition. 100 Go you, Malvolio. If it be a suit from the Count, I am

sick, or not at home. What you will, to dismiss it.

[*Exit* Malvolio

102 *old*: stale. Now you see, sir, how your fooling grows old, and

people dislike it.

Feste

Thou hast spoke for us, madonna, as if thy eldest son

104–5 *as if . . . fool*: i.e. wisely; 'A wise 105 should be a fool: whose skull Jove cram with brains! For
man often has a fool for a son'
(proverbial). here he comes, one of thy kin has a most weak *pia*

106–7 *pia mater*: brain. *mater*.

Enter Sir Toby

Olivia

By mine honour, half drunk. What is he at the gate,

cousin?

Sir Toby

110 A gentleman.

Olivia

A gentleman? What gentleman?

Sir Toby

'Tis a gentleman here—[*Belches*] A plague o' these

113 *pickle-herring*: Sir Toby tries to hide pickle-herring! How now, sot?
his drunkenness.
sot: fool; drunkard. **Feste**

Good Sir Toby!

Olivia

115 Cousin, cousin, how have you come so early by this

116 *lethargy*: drunken stupor—but Sir lethargy?
Toby wilfully mishears. **Sir Toby**

Lechery? I defy lechery. There's one at the gate.

Olivia

Ay, marry, what is he?

Sir Toby

119 *an*: if. Let him be the devil an he will, I care not: give me faith,
give me faith: i.e. as protection from
the devil; theologians debated whether 120 say I. Well, it's all one.   [*Exit*
man achieved salvation through faith
or good works.

120 *it's all one*: it doesn't matter.

Olivia
What's a drunken man like, fool?

Feste
Like a drowned man, a fool, and a madman: one draught above heat makes him a fool, the second mads him, and a third drowns him.

Olivia
125 Go thou and seek the crowner, and let him sit o' my coz: for he's in the third degree of drink—he's drowned. Go look after him.

Feste
He is but mad yet, madonna, and the fool shall look to the madman.   [*Exit*

Enter Malvolio

Malvolio
130 Madam, yond young fellow swears he will speak with you. I told him you were sick; he takes on him to understand so much, and therefore comes to speak with you. I told him you were asleep; he seems to have a foreknowledge of that too, and therefore comes to
135 speak with you. What is to be said to him, lady? He's fortified against any denial.

Olivia
Tell him, he shall not speak with me.

Malvolio
'Has been told so; and he says he'll stand at your door like a sheriff's post, and be the supporter to a bench, but
140 he'll speak with you.

Olivia
What kind o' man is he?

Malvolio
Why, of mankind.

Olivia
What manner of man?

Malvolio
Of very ill manner: he'll speak with you, will you or no.

Olivia
145 Of what personage and years is he?

123 *draught*: drink.
   above heat: beyond normal body temperature.
   mads: makes him mad.
125 *crowner*: coroner.
   sit o' my coz: hold an inquest on my kinsman.

131–2 *takes . . . much*: he says he understands that.

136 *fortified*: armed and able to resist.

138 *'Has*: he has.
139 *sheriff's post*: decorated post set (as sign of authority) before the doors of civic officials.
   supporter: prop.

142 *of mankind*: just an ordinary man.

144 *ill manner*: rude.

147 *squash*: unripe peapod ('peascod').
      codling: unripe apple.
148–9 *in standing water*: at the turn of the
      tide.
149 *well-favoured*: attractive.
150 *shrewishly*: sharply.

161 *penned*: written (i.e. composed).
162 *con*: learn by heart.
162–3 *let me . . . scorn*: don't laugh at
      me.
163 *comptible*: sensitive.
163–4 *sinister usage*: unkindness,
      discourtesy.

166 *studied*: i.e. as an actor learns his
      part.

168 *modest*: reasonable.

170 *comedian*: actor.

Malvolio
Not yet old enough for a man, nor young enough for a
boy: as a squash is before 'tis a peascod, or a codling
when 'tis almost an apple. 'Tis with him in standing
water, between boy and man. He is very well-favoured,
150 and he speaks very shrewishly. One would think his
mother's milk were scarce out of him.
    Olivia
Let him approach. Call in my gentlewoman.
    Malvolio
Gentlewoman, my lady calls.   [*Exit*

Enter Maria

    Olivia
Give me my veil: come, throw it o'er my face. We'll once
155 more hear Orsino's embassy.

Enter Viola

    Viola
The honourable lady of the house, which is she?
    Olivia
Speak to me, I shall answer for her. Your will?
    Viola
Most radiant, exquisite, and unmatchable beauty—I
pray you tell me if this be the lady of the house, for I
160 never saw her. I would be loath to cast away my speech:
for besides that it is excellently well penned, I have
taken great pains to con it. Good beauties, let me sustain
no scorn; I am very comptible, even to the least sinister
usage.
    Olivia
165 Whence came you, sir?
    Viola
I can say little more than I have studied, and that
question's out of my part. Good gentle one, give me
modest assurance if you be the lady of the house, that I
may proceed in my speech.
    Olivia
170 Are you a comedian?

171 *my . . . heart*: my wise little
  sweetheart.
171–2 *by . . . malice*: in the face of the
  most cruel spite.
172 *I am . . . play*: I am not what I
  impersonate (as the audience knows).
174 *usurp myself*: wrongfully possess my
  own person.
175–6 *you . . . reserve*: i.e. you are acting
  wrongly by not giving yourself away to
  a husband.
177 *from my commission*: not in my
  instructions.
  I will on: I will go on.

180 *forgive you*: excuse you from.

183–4 *allowed your approach*: allowed you
  to come in.

185–7 *'tis not . . . dialogue*: I am not at
  present in a mood to take part in such
  a crazy conversation.

188 *hoist sail*: prepare to leave.

189 *swabber*: cleaner of decks.
  hull: rest (with sails furled).
190 *mollification*: softener, sweetener.
  giant: Viola compares the diminutive
  Maria to the giant protectors who
  guarded the heroines of romantic
  fiction.
191 *mind*: message.
192–3 *when . . . fearful*: when you begin
  with such terrifying formality.
193 *office*: business.
194 *overture*: declaration.
195 *taxation of homage*: demand for
  tribute.
  olive: olive-branch (as a sign of
  peace).
196 *matter*: subject matter.

Viola
No, my profound heart: and yet, by the very fangs of malice, I swear, I am not that I play. Are you the lady of the house?

Olivia
If I do not usurp myself, I am.

Viola
175 Most certain, if you are she, you do usurp yourself: for what is yours to bestow is not yours to reserve. But this is from my commission. I will on with my speech in your praise, and then show you the heart of my message.

Olivia
180 Come to what is important in't: I forgive you the praise.

Viola
Alas, I took great pains to study it, and 'tis poetical.

Olivia
It is the more like to be feigned; I pray you keep it in. I heard you were saucy at my gates, and allowed your approach rather to wonder at you than to hear you. If 185 you be mad, be gone: if you have reason, be brief: 'tis not that time of moon with me to make one in so skipping a dialogue.

Maria
Will you hoist sail, sir? Here lies your way.

Viola
No, good swabber, I am to hull here a little longer. Some 190 mollification for your giant, sweet lady! Tell me your mind, I am a messenger.

Olivia
Sure you have some hideous matter to deliver, when the courtesy of it is so fearful. Speak your office.

Viola
It alone concerns your ear. I bring no overture of war, 195 no taxation of homage; I hold the olive in my hand: my words are as full of peace, as matter.

Olivia
Yet you began rudely. What are you? What would you?

199 *entertainment*: reception.
    would: want.
200 *maidenhead*: virginity.

202–13 *we will . . . text*: Olivia and Viola
    employ the diction of the secular
    'religion' of love.
202 *divinity*: sacred doctrine.
203 *text*: the subject of your discourse;
    Olivia 'catechizes' Viola (compare
    Feste, line 56).

205 *comfortable*: bringing spiritual
    consolation.

Viola
The rudeness that hath appeared in me have I learned
from my entertainment. What I am, and what I would,
200 are as secret as maidenhead: to your ears, divinity; to
any other's, profanation.
Olivia
Give us the place alone: we will hear this divinity.
                    [*Exeunt* Maria *and* Attendants
Now, sir, what is your text?
Viola
Most sweet lady—
Olivia
205 A comfortable doctrine, and much may be said of it.
Where lies your text?
Viola
In Orsino's bosom.
Olivia
In his bosom? In what chapter of his bosom?

209 *by the method*: according to the catechism.

210 *heresy*: false doctrine.

213 *out of*: departing from.

215 *this present*: just now; Olivia speaks as though her face were a picture.

217 *if . . . all*: i.e. if you haven't used cosmetics.

218 *in grain*: ingrained, natural.

219 *blent*: blended.

220 *cunning*: skilful.

221 *she*: woman.

222 *lead*: carry.

223 *copy*: i.e. a child.

224–5 *divers schedules*: various detailed listings.

226 *every . . . will*: every particularized item and furnishing added as a codicil to my will.

227 *indifferent*: fairly.
lids: eyelids.

229 *praise*: appraise, make a valuation of.

231 *if . . . devil*: even if you were as proud as Lucifer (leader of the fallen angels).

233 *Could . . . recompens'd*: would not receive more than it deserved.

233–4 *crown'd . . . beauty*: crowned the unequalled queen of beauty.

235 *fertile*: abundant.

Viola
To answer by the method, in the first of his heart.
Olivia
210 O, I have read it: it is heresy. Have you no more to say?
Viola
Good madam, let me see your face.
Olivia
Have you any commission from your lord to negotiate with my face? You are now out of your text: but we will draw the curtain and show you the picture. [*Removes
215 her veil*] Look you, sir, such a one I was this present. Is't not well done?
Viola
Excellently done, if God did all.
Olivia
'Tis in grain, sir, 'twill endure wind and weather.
Viola
'Tis beauty truly blent, whose red and white
220 Nature's own sweet and cunning hand laid on.
Lady, you are the cruell'st she alive
If you will lead these graces to the grave
And leave the world no copy.
Olivia
O sir, I will not be so hard-hearted: I will give out divers
225 schedules of my beauty. It shall be inventoried, and every particle and utensil labelled to my will. As *Item*: two lips indifferent red; *Item*: two grey eyes, with lids to them; *Item*: one neck, one chin, and so forth. Were you sent hither to praise me?
Viola
230 I see you what you are, you are too proud:
But if you were the devil, you are fair.
My lord and master loves you: O, such love
Could be but recompens'd, though you were crown'd
The nonpareil of beauty!
Olivia
How does he love me?
Viola
235 With adorations, fertile tears,
With groans that thunder love, with sighs of fire.

Olivia
Your lord does know my mind, I cannot love him.
Yet I suppose him virtuous, know him noble,
Of great estate, of fresh and stainless youth;
240 In voices well divulg'd, free, learn'd, and valiant,
And in dimension, and the shape of nature,
A gracious person: but yet I cannot love him.
He might have took his answer long ago.
Viola
If I did love you in my master's flame,
245 With such a suff'ring, such a deadly life,
In your denial I would find no sense,
I would not understand it.
Olivia
                                        Why, what would you?
Viola
Make me a willow cabin at your gate,
And call upon my soul within the house;
250 Write loyal cantons of contemnèd love,
And sing them loud even in the dead of night;
Halloo your name to the reverberate hills,
And make the babbling gossip of the air
Cry out 'Olivia!' O, you should not rest
255 Between the elements of air and earth,
But you should pity me.
Olivia
                                        You might do much.
What is your parentage?
Viola
Above my fortunes, yet my state is well:
I am a gentleman.
Olivia
                                        Get you to your lord:
260 I cannot love him: let him send no more—
Unless, perchance, you come to me again,
To tell me how he takes it. Fare you well.
I thank you for your pains, spend this for me.
Viola
I am no fee'd post, lady; keep your purse.
265 My master, not myself, lacks recompense.
Love make his heart of flint that you shall love,

---

238 *suppose him*: believe him to be.

240 *In voices well divulg'd*: well spoken of.
free: generous.
241 *in dimension . . . nature*: in his physical form.
242 *gracious*: graceful, attractive.

244 *flame*: spirit.
245 *With . . . life*: Viola pictures Orsino as a martyr, dying for love.

248 *willow cabin*: hut of willows (the emblem of unrequited love).
249 *my soul*: i.e. Olivia.
250 *cantons*: songs.
contemned: contemnèd; rejected.
252 *Halloo*: shout.
reverberate: resonant.
253 *babbling . . . air*: Echo, a nymph who wasted away for love of Narcissus until nothing remained but her voice.
254 *rest*: a) remain; b) have peace of mind.
255 *Between . . . earth*: i.e. anywhere.

257 *parentage*: family.

258 *state*: present social rank.

264 *fee'd post*: messenger who accepts tips.

266 *that*: whom.

And let your fervour like my master's be
Plac'd in contempt. Farewell, fair cruelty.   [*Exit*

Olivia
'What is your parentage?'

270 'Above my fortunes, yet my state is well;
I am a gentleman.' I'll be sworn thou art:
Thy tongue, thy face, thy limbs, actions, and spirit
Do give thee five-fold blazon. Not too fast: soft! soft!
Unless the master were the man—How now?

275 Even so quickly may one catch the plague?
Methinks I feel this youth's perfections
With an invisible and subtle stealth
To creep in at mine eyes. Well, let it be.
What ho, Malvolio!

Enter Malvolio

Malvolio

Here, madam, at your service.

Olivia
280 Run after that same peevish messenger
The County's man. He left this ring behind him,
Would I or not. Tell him, I'll none of it;
Desire him not to flatter with his lord,
Nor hold him up with hopes: I am not for him.

285 If that the youth will come this way tomorrow,
I'll give him reasons for't. Hie thee, Malvolio.

Malvolio
Madam, I will.   [*Exit*

Olivia
I do I know not what, and fear to find
Mine eye too great a flatterer for my mind.

290 Fate, show thy force; ourselves we do not owe.
What is decreed, must be: and be this so.   [*Exit*

273 *five-fold blazon*: a heraldic coat-of-arms five times over.
soft: slowly.

274 *Unless . . . man*: unless the servant were the master.

280 *peevish*: stubborn.
281 *County*: count.
282 *Would I or not*: whether or not I wanted it.
283 *flatter with*: give encouragement to.

286 *Hie thee*: hurry.

289 *Mine . . . mind*: my eyes have had too much influence over my judgement.
290 *ourselves . . . owe*: we are not our own masters.
owe: own, possess.

ACT 2

Act 2 Scene 1
Sebastian grieves for his twin sister, apparently lost in a shipwreck, and sets off to try his luck in Illyria, accompanied by Antonio.

1–2 *Nor . . . you*: do you not wish me to come with you.

3 *By your patience*: be patient with me. *My stars . . . me*: I am an unlucky person.
4 *malignancy*: bad luck (the evil influence of his stars). *distemper*: infect.

9 *sooth*: indeed. *determinate voyage*: planned course of action.
10 *extravagancy*: wandering around.
10–11 *so . . . modesty*: such good manners.
11 *extort*: demand.
12 *keep in*: keep secret.
12–13 *it charges . . . myself*: courtesy insists that I should reveal myself.
15 *Roderigo*: No explanation is ever given for Sebastian's earlier use of an alias. *Messaline*: a town invented by Shakespeare.
17 *in*: within.
19 *some hour*: about an hour.
20 *breach*: surf.

23 *was*: who was.

24 *estimable wonder*: admiring judgement. *overfar*: too far.
25 *publish her*: describe.

SCENE 1

The sea coast: enter Antonio *and* Sebastian

Antonio
Will you stay no longer? Nor will you not that I go with you?

Sebastian
By your patience, no. My stars shine darkly over me; the malignancy of my fate might perhaps distemper yours, 5 therefore I shall crave of you your leave that I may bear my evils alone. It were a bad recompense for your love, to lay any of them on you.

Antonio
Let me yet know of you whither you are bound.

Sebastian
No, sooth, sir: my determinate voyage is mere 10 extravagancy. But I perceive in you so excellent a touch of modesty, that you will not extort from me what I am willing to keep in; therefore it charges me in manners the rather to express myself. You must know of me then, Antonio, my name is Sebastian, which I called 15 Roderigo; my father was that Sebastian of Messaline whom I know you have heard of. He left behind him myself and a sister, both born in an hour; if the heavens had been pleased, would we had so ended! But you, sir, altered that, for some hour before you took me from the 20 breach of the sea was my sister drowned.

Antonio
Alas the day!

Sebastian
A lady, sir, though it was said she much resembled me, was yet of many accounted beautiful. But though I could not with such estimable wonder overfar believe 25 that, yet thus far I will boldly publish her: she bore a mind that envy could not but call fair. She is drowned

28 *remembrance*: memory.
    with more: i.e. with tears.

29 *your . . . entertainment*: my poor
    hospitality.

30 *your trouble*: for giving you such
    trouble.

31 *If . . . me*: if you don't want to cause
    me to die of grief (by leaving me).

34 *recovered*: saved.
    desire: request.
35 *kindness*: emotion.
    yet: still.
36 *manners of my mother*: the behaviour
    of a woman.
37 *tell . . . me*: betray me (by weeping).
38 *bound*: going.

Act 2 Scene 2
Malvolio gives Olivia's ring to Viola—who
immediately understands what has
happened.

0s.d. *at several doors*: at different
       entrances.
1 *ev'n*: just.

2 *on . . . pace*: walking reasonably fast.

3 *but hither*: only here.

7 *desperate assurance*: certainty that
   there is no hope.
8 *so hardy*: so bold as to.
9–10 *taking of this*: response to (a) this
      ultimatum; (b) this ring.
10 *Receive it so*: take the ring on this
    understanding.

already, sir, with salt water, though I seem to drown her
remembrance again with more.

Antonio
Pardon me, sir, your bad entertainment.

Sebastian
30 O good Antonio, forgive me your trouble.

Antonio
If you will not murder me for my love, let me be your
servant.

Sebastian
If you will not undo what you have done—that is, kill
35 him whom you have recovered—desire it not. Fare ye
well at once; my bosom is full of kindness, and I am yet
so near the manners of my mother that upon the least
occasion more mine eyes will tell tales of me. I am
bound to the Count Orsino's court. Farewell.   [*Exit*

Antonio
The gentleness of all the gods go with thee!
40 I have many enemies in Orsino's court,
Else would I very shortly see thee there.
But come what may, I do adore thee so
That danger shall seem sport, and I will go.   [*Exit*

Scene 2

A street: enter Viola *and* Malvolio, *at several doors*

Malvolio
Were not you ev'n now with the Countess Olivia?

Viola
Even now, sir; on a moderate pace I have since arrived
but hither.

Malvolio
She returns this ring to you, sir. You might have saved
5 me my pains, to have taken it away yourself. She adds,
moreover, that you should put your lord into a
desperate assurance she will none of him. And one
thing more, that you be never so hardy to come again in
his affairs, unless it be to report your lord's taking of
10 this. Receive it so.

11 *of*: from.

12 *peevishly*: rudely.
threw it: Malvolio elaborates: Olivia simply said that he 'left it' (*1*, 5, 281).
14 *in your eye*: in plain sight.

17 *outside*: appearance (in male attire).
18 *made good view of*: looked hard at.

20 *in starts*: brokenly, not in complete sentences.

22 *in*: through, by means of.

24 *the man*: whom she has chosen.

27 *pregnant*: full of ideas.
enemy: Satan, the 'enemy of mankind' (who is always disguised).
28 *proper false*: handsome deceivers.
29 *waxen*: easily impressed.
set their forms: imprint themselves (as a seal is imprinted on wax).
30 *the cause*: i.e. of women's susceptibility to love.
31 *such . . . be*: we are what we are made of; Viola excuses her own weakness, as well as Olivia's.
32 *fadge*: turn out.
33 *monster*: i.e. because both male and female.
fond: dote.
35 *As . . . man*: since I am disguised as a man.
36 *desperate*: hopeless.
38 *thriftless*: wasted, unprofitable.

Viola
She took the ring of me. I'll none of it.
        Malvolio
Come sir, you peevishly threw it to her; and her will is,
it should be so returned. If it be worth stooping for,
there it lies [*throws down the ring*] in your eye; or if not,
15 be it his that finds it.   [*Exit*
        Viola
I left no ring with her: what means this lady?
Fortune forbid my outside have not charm'd her!
She made good view of me, indeed so much
That methought her eyes had lost her tongue,
20 For she did speak in starts, distractedly.
She loves me, sure; the cunning of her passion
Invites me in this churlish messenger.
None of my lord's ring? Why, he sent her none.
I am the man! If it be so, as 'tis,
25 Poor lady, she were better love a dream.
Disguise, I see thou art a wickedness
Wherein the pregnant enemy does much.
How easy is it for the proper false
In women's waxen hearts to set their forms!
30 Alas, our frailty is the cause, not we:
For such as we are made of, such we be.
How will this fadge? My master loves her dearly;
And I, poor monster, fond as much on him;
And she, mistaken, seems to dote on me.
35 What will become of this? As I am man,
My state is desperate for my master's love:
As I am woman (now alas the day!)
What thriftless sighs shall poor Olivia breathe?
O time, thou must untangle this, not I:
40 It is too hard a knot for me t'untie.   [*Exit*

Act 2 Scene 3
Although Maria gives them a warning, the drunken revelry of Sir Toby and his friends incurs the wrath of Malvolio—but Maria plans retaliation.

2   *betimes*: early.
diluculo surgere: Sir Toby quotes part of a Latin sentence found in all sixteenth-century Latin grammars: *diliculo surgere saluberrimum est*—to rise early is very healthy.
3   *troth*: faith.
5   *conclusion*: reasoning.
can: drinking vessel.

8   *the four elements*: fire, air, water, and earth; these were believed to compose all matter and, differently compounded in the human body, to give rise to four 'humours' (choler, blood, phlegm, and black bile) which determined temperament and appearance.
11   *Marian*: Maria.
12   *stoup*: jug.

14–15   *picture . . . three'*: a sign-board representing two fools or asses, inscribed 'We Three'—the spectator being the third.
16   *ass*: Sir Toby responds to Feste's joke.
catch: round, part-song.

17   *breast*: singing-voice.
17–19   *I had . . . has*: I would pay a lot of money ('forty' = a large, but non-specific, amount) to be able to dance and sing as well as the fool.

21–2   *Pigrogromitus . . . Vapians . . . Queubus*: the names are invented; Feste was obviously telling some fantastic traveller's tale.
21   *equinoctial*: equator.
23   *leman*: sweetheart.

SCENE 3

Olivia's house: enter Sir Toby *and* Sir Andrew

Sir Toby
Approach, Sir Andrew. Not to be abed after midnight, is to be up betimes; and *diluculo surgere*, thou know'st—
Sir Andrew
Nay, by my troth, I know not; but I know, to be up late, is to be up late.
Sir Toby
5   A false conclusion! I hate it as an unfilled can. To be up after midnight, and to go to bed then, is early; so that to go to bed after midnight is to go to bed betimes. Does not our life consist of the four elements?
Sir Andrew
Faith, so they say; but I think it rather consists of eating
10   and drinking.
Sir Toby
Th'art a scholar; let us therefore eat and drink. Marian, I say! A stoup of wine!

Enter Feste

Sir Andrew
Here comes the fool, i' faith.
Feste
How now, my hearts? Did you never see the picture of
15   'we three'?
Sir Toby
Welcome, ass. Now let's have a catch.
Sir Andrew
By my troth, the fool has an excellent breast. I had rather than forty shillings I had such a leg, and so sweet a breath to sing, as the fool has. In sooth, thou wast in
20   very gracious fooling last night, when thou spok'st of Pigrogromitus, of the Vapians passing the equinoctial of Queubus. 'Twas very good, i' faith. I sent thee sixpence for thy leman: hadst it?

24–6 *I did . . . houses*: Feste is fooling.
24 *impeticos thy gratillity*: pocket your little tip (Feste creates his own language).
25 *whipstock*: whip-handle.
26 *Myrmidons*: followers of the Greek warrior Achilles.

30 *testril*: sixpence.
a—: The line ends at the margin in the Folio text, and it seems that the printer has missed some words.
31 *song . . . life*: i.e. a pastoral song, preferring the life of a shepherd to court life.

34 *O mistress mine*: See Appendix, p.103.

42 *'Tis not hereafter*: it is not something for the future.

44 *still*: always.

45 *plenty*: profit, advantage.

46 *sweet and twenty*: sweet and twenty times sweet (a term of endearment).

48 *mellifluous*: honey-sweet.

49 *contagious breath*: catchy tune (with a play on 'contagious' = infectious).

Feste
I did impeticos thy gratillity: for Malvolio's nose is no
25 whipstock, my lady has a white hand, and the
Myrmidons are no bottle-ale houses.
Sir Andrew
Excellent! Why, this is the best fooling, when all is done.
Now a song!
Sir Toby
Come on, there is sixpence for you. Let's have a song.
Sir Andrew
30 There's a testril of me too; if one knight give a—
Feste
Would you have a love-song, or a song of good life?
Sir Toby
A love-song, a love-song!
Sir Andrew
Ay, ay. I care not for good life.
Feste
O mistress mine, where are you roaming?
35 *O stay and hear, your true love's coming,*
That can sing both high and low.
Trip no further, pretty sweeting:
Journeys end in lovers meeting,
Every wise man's son doth know.
Sir Andrew
40 Excellent good, i' faith.
Sir Toby
Good, good.
Feste
What is love? 'Tis not hereafter,
Present mirth hath present laughter:
What's to come is still unsure.
45 *In delay there lies no plenty,*
Then come kiss me, sweet and twenty,
Youth's a stuff will not endure.
Sir Andrew
A mellifluous voice, as I am a true knight.
Sir Toby
A contagious breath.
Sir Andrew
50 Very sweet and contagious, i' faith.

51 *To hear by the nose*: if we hear the tune with our noses (as we catch the smell of breath).
   dulcet in contagion: sweet in its infection.
52 *make . . . dance*: drink until the sky ('welkin') spins round.
53–4 *draw . . . weaver*: Music was said to draw the soul out of the body—but the songs sung by weavers (often Calvinist refugees from the Low Countries) were usually psalms.
55 *An*: if.
   dog: adept, expert.
56 *By'r lady*: by Our Lady.
   dogs: mechanical gripping devices.
57 *'Thou knave'*: In this round-song ('Hold thy peace, thou knave, and I prithee hold thy peace'), each of the singers in turn is called 'knave'.

61 *'Hold thy peace'*: be silent.

65 *called up*: sent for.
66 *out of doors*: out of the house.
67 *Cataian*: Chinese (from Cathay), villain; this is more of Sir Toby's nonsense.
   politicians: men of craft and cunning.
67–8 *Peg-a-Ramsey*: a character in a popular song.
68 *Three . . . we*: a phrase found in several Elizabethan songs.
69 *consanguineous*: of the same blood, related (to Olivia).
   Tilly-vally: fiddle-faddle!; an expression of impatience.
70 *There . . . Lady*: The first line of a popular ballad about Susannah and the Elders.
71 *Beshrew me*: a mild oath.

Sir Toby
To hear by the nose, it is dulcet in contagion. But shall we make the welkin dance indeed? Shall we rouse the night-owl in a catch that will draw three souls out of one weaver? Shall we do that?

Sir Andrew
55 An you love me, let's do't: I am dog at a catch.

Feste
By'r lady, sir, and some dogs will catch well.

Sir Andrew
Most certain. Let our catch be 'Thou knave'.

Feste
'Hold thy peace, thou knave', knight? I shall be constrained in't to call thee knave, knight.

Sir Andrew
60 'Tis not the first time I have constrained one to call me knave. Begin, fool; it begins; [*sings*] 'Hold thy peace'.

Feste
I shall never begin if I hold my peace.

Sir Andrew
Good, i' faith. Come, begin.

They join in the singing

Enter Maria

Maria
What a caterwauling do you keep here? If my lady have
65 not called up her steward Malvolio and bid him turn you out of doors, never trust me.

Sir Toby
My lady's a Cataian, we are politicians, Malvolio's a Peg-a-Ramsey, and [*Sings*] *Three merry men be we*. Am I not consanguineous? Am I not of her blood? Tilly-vally!
70 'Lady!' [*Sings*] *There dwelt a man in Babylon, Lady, Lady.*

Feste
Beshrew me, the knight's in admirable fooling.

Sir Andrew
Ay, he does well enough, if he be disposed, and so do I

74 *natural*: naturally, like a born idiot.

75 *O' . . . December*: Shakespeare may have altered a well-known line for the special occasion of the play.

too: he does it with a better grace, but I do it more natural.

Sir Toby
75 *O' the twelfth day of December—*
Maria
For the love o' God, peace!

Enter Malvolio

Malvolio
My masters, are you mad? Or what are you? Have you no wit, manners, nor honesty, but to gabble like tinkers at this time of night? Do ye make an ale-house of my 80 lady's house, that ye squeak out your coziers' catches without any mitigation or remorse of voice? Is there no respect of place, persons, nor time in you?

78 *wit . . . honesty*: judgement, breeding, decency.

80 *coziers*: cobblers.

81 *mitigation*: consideration.
remorse of voice: lowering your voices.

'My masters, are you mad?' (*2*, 3, 77) Gemma Jones as Maria, Emrys James as Malvolio, and Stephen Moore as Sir Toby Belch, Royal Shakespeare Company, 1984.

83 *Sneck up*: go away.

84 *round*: blunt.

86 *nothing allied*: not related.

90–100 Sir Toby and Feste sing a song
first published in 1600, adapting the
words to suit their own situation.

101 *Out o' time*: Sir Toby reverts to
Malvolio's accusation of line 82.
102 *virtuous*: strictly religious and narrow-
minded.
103 *cakes and ale*: festivities with eating
and drinking.
104 *Saint Anne*: the mother of the Virgin
Mary—an oath offensive to Puritan
ears.
ginger: used to spice the ale.

106 *rub . . . crumbs*: polish your steward's
chain (his badge of office—and a
reminder that he is only a servant).

Sir Toby
We did keep time, sir, in our catches. Sneck up!

Malvolio
Sir Toby, I must be round with you. My lady bade me
85 tell you that, though she harbours you as her kinsman,
she's nothing allied to your disorders. If you can
separate yourself and your misdemeanours, you are
welcome to the house: if not, and it would please you to
take leave of her, she is very willing to bid you farewell.

Sir Toby
90 *Farewell, dear heart, since I must needs be gone.*

Maria
Nay, good Sir Toby.

Feste
His eyes do show his days are almost done.

Malvolio
Is't even so?

Sir Toby
But I will never die.

Feste
95 *Sir Toby, there you lie.*

Malvolio
This is much credit to you.

Sir Toby
Shall I bid him go?

Feste
What and if you do?

Sir Toby
Shall I bid him go, and spare not?

Feste
100 *O no, no, no, no, you dare not.*

Sir Toby
Out o' time, sir? ye lie! Art any more than a steward?
Dost thou think, because thou art virtuous, there shall
be no more cakes and ale?

Feste
Yes, by Saint Anne, and ginger shall be hot i' th' mouth
105 too.   [*Exit*

Sir Toby
Th'art i' th' right. Go sir, rub your chain with crumbs. A
stoup of wine, Maria!

Malvolio

Mistress Mary, if you prized my lady's favour at anything more than contempt, you would not give
110 means for this uncivil rule. She shall know of it, by this hand.   [*Exit*

Maria

Go shake your ears.

Sir Andrew

'Twere as good a deed as to drink when a man's a-hungry, to challenge him the field and then to break
115 promise with him and make a fool of him.

Sir Toby

Do't, knight. I'll write thee a challenge; or I'll deliver thy indignation to him by word of mouth.

Maria

Sweet Sir Toby, be patient for tonight. Since the youth of the Count's was today with my lady, she is much out of
120 quiet. For Monsieur Malvolio, let me alone with him. If I do not gull him into a nayword, and make him a common recreation, do not think I have wit enough to lie straight in my bed. I know I can do it.

Sir Toby

Possess us, possess us, tell us something of him.

Maria

125 Marry sir, sometimes he is a kind of Puritan.

Sir Andrew

O, if I thought that, I'd beat him like a dog.

Sir Toby

What, for being a Puritan? Thy exquisite reason, dear knight?

Sir Andrew

I have no exquisite reason for't, but I have reason good
130 enough.

Maria

The devil a Puritan that he is, or anything constantly, but a time-pleaser, an affectioned ass that cons state without book, and utters it by great swarths; the best persuaded of himself, so crammed (as he thinks) with
135 excellencies, that it is his grounds of faith that all that look on him love him: and on that vice in him will my revenge find notable cause to work.

112 *Go . . . ears*: a common insult, often accompanied with a gesture suggesting that the hearer has the long ears of an ass.
113 *as good . . . drink*: it would be an excellent idea (a common phrase).
114 *the field*: to a duel.

119–20 *out of quiet*: disturbed.
120 *let . . . him*: leave him to me.
121 *gull . . . nayword*: deceive him so that his name becomes synonymous with 'fool'.
122 *recreation*: source of amusement.

124 *Possess us*: tell us, let us know your idea.
125 *kind of Puritan*: i.e. morally narrow-minded, but not a member of any specific religious sect.

132 *time-pleaser*: time-server.
      affectioned: affected.
132–3 *cons . . . book*: learns the rules of etiquette by heart.
133 *swarths*: swathes (literally, the amount of corn cut down with a sweep of the scythe).
133–4 *the best persuaded*: having the highest opinion.
135 *grounds of faith*: belief.

139 *obscure*: ambiguously-worded.

141 *expressure*: expression.

143 *feelingly personated*: fully described.
144 *a forgotten matter*: something that we
have forgotten.
144–5 *make distinction of*: tell the
difference between.
145 *hands*: handwriting.
146 *smell a device*: begin to understand
the trick.

148 *by*: from.

151 *a horse of that colour*: something of
that kind (a proverbial expression).

152 *Ass*: Maria puns on 'ass' and 'as'.

155 *Sport royal*: fun fit for a king.
physic: medicine.

158 *construction*: interpretation.

160 *Penthesilea*: queen of the warlike race
of Amazons; Sir Toby teases the tiny
Maria as well as praising her wit.
161 *Before me*: upon my soul.

162 *beagle*: small hound.

Sir Toby
What wilt thou do?
Maria
I will drop in his way some obscure epistles of love,
140 wherein by the colour of his beard, the shape of his leg,
the manner of his gait, the expressure of his eye,
forehead, and complexion, he shall find himself most
feelingly personated. I can write very like my lady your
niece; on a forgotten matter we can hardly make
145 distinction of our hands.
Sir Toby
Excellent! I smell a device.
Sir Andrew
I have't in my nose too.
Sir Toby
He shall think by the letters that thou wilt drop that
they come from my niece, and that she's in love with
150 him.
Maria
My purpose is indeed a horse of that colour.
Sir Andrew
And your horse now would make him an ass.
Maria
Ass, I doubt not.
Sir Andrew
O, 'twill be admirable!
Maria
155 Sport royal, I warrant you: I know my physic will work
with him. I will plant you two, and let the fool make a
third, where he shall find the letter. Observe his
construction of it. For this night, to bed, and dream on
the event. Farewell.   [*Exit*
Sir Toby
160 Good night, Penthesilea.
Sir Andrew
Before me, she's a good wench.
Sir Toby
She's a beagle, true-bred, and one that adores me—
what o' that?
Sir Andrew
I was adored once too.

Sir Toby

165 Let's to bed, knight. Thou hadst need send for more money.

Sir Andrew

If I cannot recover your niece, I am a foul way out.

Sir Toby

Send for money, knight. If thou hast her not i' th' end, call me cut.

Sir Andrew

170 If I do not, never trust me, take it how you will.

Sir Toby

Come, come, I'll go burn some sack, 'tis too late to go to bed now. Come, knight; come, knight.   [*Exeunt*

SCENE 4

The Duke'*s court: enter* Orsino, Viola, Curio, *and others*

Orsino

Give me some music. Now good morrow, friends.
Now, good Cesario, but that piece of song,
That old and antic song we heard last night;
Methought it did relieve my passion much,
5 More than light airs and recollected terms
Of these most brisk and giddy-paced times.
Come, but one verse.

Curio

He is not here, so please your lordship, that should sing it.

Orsino

10 Who was it?

Curio

Feste the jester, my lord, a fool that the Lady Olivia's father took much delight in. He is about the house.

Orsino

Seek him out, and play the tune the while.
                    [*Exit* Curio. *Music plays*
Come hither, boy. If ever thou shalt love,
15 In the sweet pangs of it remember me.

---

167 *recover*: obtain (and recoup his expenses).
  a foul way out: grievously out of pocket.
169 *cut*: gelding (a castrated horse).

171 *burn . . . sack*: heat up some white wine with sugar.

Act 2 Scene 4
Orsino explains the nature of love to Viola/Cesario.

0s.d. *others*: These should include musicians, as well as attendant lords.

1 *morrow*: morning.
2 *but*: only.
3 *antic*: quaint.
4 *Methought*: I thought.
5 *recollected terms*: elaborate musical phrases.
6 *paced*: pacèd.

17 *Unstaid*: unsure.
   skittish: playful.
   all motions else: all other emotions.
18 *image*: idea.

20 *the seat*: i.e. the heart.

22 *My life upon't*: I would bet my life
   upon it.
23 *stay'd*: looked, rested.
   favour: face.

24 *by your favour*: if I may say so (with a
   pun on 'favour' in line 23).

25 *Of your complexion*: rather like you.

28 *still*: always.

30 *sways . . . heart*: her love holds an
   equal balance with her husband's.

32–4 *Our . . . are*: Orsino contradicts his
   earlier claims (lines 16–19).
32 *fancies*: loves.
33 *worn*: exhausted.

36 *hold the bent*: stand the strain; 'bent'
   = the extent to which a bow can be
   made taut.
38 *display'd*: opened in full bloom.

40 *even*: just.

For such as I am, all true lovers are:
Unstaid and skittish in all motions else
Save in the constant image of the creature
That is belov'd. How dost thou like this tune?
    Viola
20 It gives a very echo to the seat
Where love is thron'd.
    Orsino
                    Thou dost speak masterly.
My life upon't, young though thou art, thine eye
Hath stay'd upon some favour that it loves.
Hath it not, boy?
    Viola
                 A little, by your favour.
    Orsino
25 What kind of woman is't?
    Viola
                    Of your complexion.
    Orsino
She is not worth thee then. What years, i' faith?
    Viola
About your years, my lord.
    Orsino
Too old, by heaven! Let still the woman take
An elder than herself; so wears she to him,
30 So sways she level in her husband's heart:
For boy, however we do praise ourselves,
Our fancies are more giddy and unfirm,
More longing, wavering, sooner lost and worn
Than women's are.
    Viola
               I think it well, my lord.
    Orsino
35 Then let thy love be younger than thyself,
Or thy affection cannot hold the bent.
For women are as roses, whose fair flower
Being once display'd, doth fall that very hour.
    Viola
And so they are: alas, that they are so.
40 To die, even when they to perfection grow!

42 *Mark it*: listen to it.

43 *spinsters*: spinners.

44 *free*: carefree.
weave . . . bones: make lace (using bobbins made of bone).

45 *Do . . . it*: often sing it.
silly sooth: simple truth.

46 *dallies*: sports, plays.

47 *Like the old age*: as they did in the old days.

50 *Come away*: come quickly to me.

51 *cypress*: coffin of cypress wood.

52 *Fie away*: be off.

54 *stuck . . . yew*: covered over with yew leaves.

56–7 *My . . . share it*: no such constant lover ever died for love.

66 *pains*: troubles (i.e. in singing).

Enter Curio *and* Feste

Orsino
O, fellow, come, the song we had last night.
Mark it, Cesario—it is old and plain;
The spinsters and the knitters in the sun,
And the free maids that weave their threads with bones
45 Do use to chant it: it is silly sooth,
And dallies with the innocence of love,
Like the old age.
Feste
Are you ready, sir?
Orsino
Ay, prithee sing.

Music

Feste
50 *Come away, come away death,*
And in sad cypress let me be laid.
Fie away, fie away breath,
I am slain by a fair cruel maid:
My shroud of white, stuck all with yew,
55 *O prepare it.*
My part of death no one so true
Did share it.

Not a flower, not a flower sweet,
On my black coffin let there be strewn:
60 *Not a friend, not a friend greet*
My poor corpse, where my bones shall be thrown:
A thousand thousand sighs to save,
Lay me, O where
Sad true lover never find my grave,
65 *To weep there.*

Orsino
There's for thy pains. [*Gives him money*]
Feste
No pains, sir, I take pleasure in singing, sir.
Orsino
I'll pay thy pleasure then.

69 *pleasure . . . another*: Feste alludes to the proverbial notion that pleasure must be paid for with pain.

70 *Give . . . thee*: Orsino dismisses Feste with wit and courtesy.

71 *the melancholy god*: Saturn, whose planetary influence shed gloom on those born under it.

72 *doublet*: sleeveless jacket. *changeable taffeta*: iridescent silk.

73 *opal*: a semi-precious stone which changes colour in different lights.

73-4 *I . . . sea*: I think men like you should become sea-merchants.

74-5 *that . . . everywhere*: so that they could deal in everything and trade everywhere.

75 *intent*: port of call.

75-6 *that's . . . nothing*: that's the way to make a profitable business from nothing.

77 *give place*: take themselves away.

78 *yond*: yonder. *sovereign cruelty*: queen of cruelty.

79 *than the world*: than any other in the world.

81 *The parts*: i.e. the wealth and social status.

82 *hold*: value. *giddily*: lightly, carelessly; Fortune is fickle in her distribution of worldly goods.

83 *that . . . gems*: i.e. her beauty.

84 *pranks her in*: adorns her with.

86 *Sooth*: indeed.

92 *bide*: endure.

94 *retention*: the ability to retain (a medical term).

95 *appetite*: desire, lust.

96 *No . . . liver*: not an emotion arising out of the liver (thought to be the seat of love).

97 *That . . . revolt*: that can be surfeited, cloyed, and revolted (by over-eating).

Feste
Truly sir, and pleasure will be paid, one time or another.

Orsino
70 Give me now leave to leave thee.

Feste
Now the melancholy god protect thee, and the tailor make thy doublet of changeable taffeta, for thy mind is a very opal. I would have men of such constancy put to sea, that their business might be everything, and their
75 intent everywhere, for that's it that always makes a good voyage of nothing. Farewell.   [*Exit*

Orsino
Let all the rest give place.
                              [*Exeunt* Curio, *and* Attendants
                              Once more, Cesario,
Get thee to yond same sovereign cruelty.
Tell her my love, more noble than the world,
80 Prizes not quantity of dirty lands:
The parts that fortune hath bestow'd upon her,
Tell her I hold as giddily as fortune.
But 'tis that miracle and queen of gems
That nature pranks her in, attracts my soul.

Viola
85 But if she cannot love you, sir?

Orsino
I cannot be so answer'd.

Viola
                              Sooth, but you must.
Say that some lady—as perhaps there is—
Hath for your love as great a pang of heart
As you have for Olivia: you cannot love her;
90 You tell her so. Must she not then be answer'd?

Orsino
There is no woman's sides
Can bide the beating of so strong a passion
As love doth give my heart; no woman's heart
So big, to hold so much. They lack retention.
95 Alas, their love may be call'd appetite,
No motion of the liver, but the palate,
That suffers surfeit, cloyment, and revolt;
But mine is all as hungry as the sea,

And can digest as much. Make no compare
100 Between that love a woman can bear me
And that I owe Olivia.

Viola

Ay, but I know—

Orsino

What dost thou know?

Viola

Too well what love women to men may owe.
In faith, they are as true of heart as we.
105 My father had a daughter lov'd a man—
As it might be, perhaps, were I a woman,
I should your lordship.

Orsino

And what's her history?

Viola

108 *a blank*: a blank page.

109 *concealment . . . bud*: secrecy like a canker-worm destroying a budding rose from the inside.

110 *damask*: blended red and white. *thought*: sadness.

111 *with . . . melancholy*: pale and sick with misery.

112–13 *like . . . grief*: like the smiling figure of Patience cut on a tombstone.

115 *Our . . . will*: we show greater passion than we feel. *still*: always.

A blank, my lord. She never told her love,
But let concealment, like a worm i' th' bud,
110 Feed on her damask cheek. She pin'd in thought,
And with a green and yellow melancholy
She sat like Patience on a monument,
Smiling at grief. Was not this love indeed?
We men may say more, swear more, but indeed
115 Our shows are more than will: for still we prove
Much in our vows, but little in our love.

Orsino

But died thy sister of her love, my boy?

Viola

I am all the daughters of my father's house,
And all the brothers too: and yet I know not.
120 Sir, shall I to this lady?

Orsino

Ay, that's the theme.

120 *shall I to*: shall I go to. *theme*: business.

122 *give no place*: not be held back. *bide no denay*: accept no refusal.

To her in haste; give her this jewel; say
My love can give no place, bide no denay.   [*Exeunt*

Act 2 Scene 5
Sir Toby and his friends watch Malvolio as he reads the letter Maria has written.

0s.d. *Fabian*: Fabian will take the place that Maria assigned to Feste (*2*, 3, 156–7).

1 *Come thy ways*: come along.

2 *a scruple*: a very tiny part.

3 *boiled*: Fabian's pronunciation ('biled') puns on the 'black bile' that was said to cause melancholy (see *2*, 3, 8 note).

5 *sheep-biter*: dissembler.
come . . . shame: be disgraced.

7 *a bear-baiting*: A popular 'sport' in which a bear, tethered to a post, was tormented by dogs.

8–9 *fool . . . blue*: bruise him with fooling.

10 *An'*: and (= if).
it is . . . lives: we don't deserve to live.

11–12 *my . . . India*: my precious pure gold.

13 *box-tree*: an evergreen shrub used for garden hedges.

14–15 *practising . . . shadow*: rehearsing gestures, using his shadow as a looking glass.

15 *this half hour*: for the past half hour.

17 *contemplative*: self-deceiving.
Close: hide and keep quiet.

20 *tickling*: flattery (as poachers catch trout by tickling them).

SCENE 5

Olivia's garden: enter Sir Toby, Sir Andrew, *and* Fabian

Sir Toby
Come thy ways, Signior Fabian.

Fabian
Nay, I'll come. If I lose a scruple of this sport, let me be boiled to death with melancholy.

Sir Toby
Would'st thou not be glad to have the niggardly rascally
5 sheep-biter come by some notable shame?

Fabian
I would exult, man: you know he brought me out o' favour with my lady about a bear-baiting here.

Sir Toby
To anger him we'll have the bear again, and we will fool him black and blue—shall we not, Sir Andrew?

Sir Andrew
10 An' we do not, it is pity of our lives.

Enter Maria

Sir Toby
Here comes the little villain. How now, my metal of India?

Maria
Get ye all three into the box-tree. Malvolio's coming down this walk; he has been yonder i' the sun practising
15 behaviour to his own shadow this half hour. Observe him, for the love of mockery; for I know this letter will make a contemplative idiot of him. Close, in the name of jesting! [*The men hide*. Maria *drops a letter*] Lie thou there, for here comes the trout that must be caught with
20 tickling. [*Exit*

Enter Malvolio

Malvolio

'Tis but fortune, all is fortune. Maria once told me she did affect me, and I have heard herself come thus near, that should she fancy, it should be one of my complexion. Besides, she uses me with a more exalted
25 respect than any one else that follows her. What should I think on't?

Sir Toby

Here's an overweening rogue!

Fabian

O, peace! Contemplation makes a rare turkey-cock of him: how he jets under his advanced plumes!

Sir Andrew

30 'Slight, I could so beat the rogue!

Sir Toby

Peace, I say!

Malvolio

To be Count Malvolio!

Sir Toby

Ah, rogue!

Sir Andrew

Pistol him, pistol him!

Sir Toby

35 Peace, peace!

Malvolio

There is example for't. The Lady of the Strachy married the yeoman of the wardrobe.

Sir Andrew

Fie on him, Jezebel!

Fabian

O peace! Now he's deeply in. Look how imagination
40 blows him.

Malvolio

Having been three months married to her, sitting in my state—

Sir Toby

O for a stone-bow to hit him in the eye!

21 *she*: i.e. Olivia.
22 *affect*: care for.
23 *fancy*: love.
23–4 *one . . . complexion*: someone like me in appearance and temperament.
24 *uses*: treats.
25 *follows*: serves.

28 *Contemplation*: conceit.
29 *jets*: struts.
  advanced: outspread.
30 *'Slight*: by God's light.

36 *example*: precedent.
36–7 *The . . . wardrobe*: An inexplicable joke with perhaps topical significance: William Strachey was a shareholder in a rival theatre, and David Yeomans was a wardrobe-keeper for the same company.
38 *Jezebel*: the proud wife of King Ahab (2 Kings 9:30–7).
40 *blows*: swells.

42 *state*: chair of state.

43 *stone-bow*: crossbow which fired stones.

'To be Count Malvolio!' (*2*, 5, 32) Eric Porter as Malvolio, Playhouse Theatre, London, 1991.

Malvolio

Calling my officers about me, in my branched velvet
45 gown, having come from a day-bed, where I have left
Olivia sleeping—

    Sir Toby

Fire and brimstone!

    Fabian

O peace, peace!

    Malvolio

And then to have the humour of state; and after a
50 demure travel of regard, telling them I know my place,
as I would they should do theirs, to ask for my kinsman
Toby.

    Sir Toby

Bolts and shackles!

    Fabian

O peace, peace, peace! Now, now!

    Malvolio

55 Seven of my people with an obedient start make out for
him. I frown the while, and perchance wind up my
watch, or play with my [*Touching his chain*]—some rich
jewel. Toby approaches; curtsies there to me—

    Sir Toby

Shall this fellow live?

    Fabian

60 Though our silence be drawn from us with cars, yet
peace!

    Malvolio

I extend my hand to him thus, quenching my familiar
smile with a austere regard of control—

    Sir Toby

And does not Toby take you a blow o' the lips then?

    Malvolio

65 Saying, 'Cousin Toby, my fortunes having cast me on
your niece give me this prerogative of speech'.

    Sir Toby

What, what?

    Malvolio

'You must amend your drunkenness.'

    Sir Toby

Out, scab!

---

44 *branched*: embroidered (with a design of tree-branches).
45 *day-bed*: couch.

49 *to have . . . state*: to adopt the grand manner.
50 *demure . . . regard*: serious look around at those present.
51–2 *my kinsman Toby*: Malvolio speaks with familiarity, neglecting to say 'Sir Toby'.
53 *Bolts and shackles*: fetters.

55 *with . . . start*: jumping obediently to attention.
    make out for: go off to find.
56 *the while*: during the meantime.
57–8 *my . . . jewel*: Malvolio suddenly remembers that in his new role he will not wear the steward's chain of office.
58 *curtsies*: bows down low.

60 *with cars*: with chariots, by force.

63 *austere . . . control*: stern look of authority.

64 *take*: give.

69 *scab*: a term of abuse.

70 *break the sinews*: cut the hamstrings, disable.

71 *treasure of your time*: your valuable time.

76 *employment*: business.
77 *woodcock*: a proverbially foolish bird. *gin*: trap, snare.
78–9 *the spirit . . . him*: may some whimsical impulse inspire him to read it aloud.
80 *hand*: handwriting.
81 *her . . . T's*: Malvolio spells out a slang word for the female genitalia.
82 *makes . . . P's*: i.e. urinates; the joke is unmistakable when the words are spoken.
    in . . . question: beyond all doubt.
86 *Soft*: gently.
87 *impressure . . . seal*: the picture of Lucrece which she usually stamps on her letters.

Lucrece: a Roman matron who committed suicide when she was violated by Tarquin; her story is told in Shakespeare's narrative poem *The Rape of Lucrece*.

89 *liver and all*: to the heart of his passion.

Fabian

70 Nay, patience, or we break the sinews of our plot.

Malvolio

'Besides, you waste the treasure of your time with a foolish knight.'

Sir Andrew

That's me, I warrant you.

Malvolio

'One Sir Andrew.'

Sir Andrew

75 I knew 'twas I, for many do call me fool.

Malvolio

[*Seeing the letter*] What employment have we here?

Fabian

Now is the woodcock near the gin.

Sir Toby

O peace! And the spirit of humours intimate reading aloud to him!

Malvolio

80 [*Picking up the letter*] By my life, this is my lady's hand: these be her very C's, her U's, and her T's, and thus makes she her great P's. It is in contempt of question her hand.

Sir Andrew

Her C's, her U's, and her T's: why that?

Malvolio

85 [*Reads*] *To the unknown beloved, this, and my good wishes.* Her very phrases! By your leave, wax. Soft! and the impressure her Lucrece, with which she uses to seal. 'Tis my lady! To whom should this be?

He opens the letter

Fabian

This wins him, liver and all.

Malvolio

90 [*Reads*]   *Jove knows I love;*
              But who?
              Lips, do not move,
              No man must know.

Act 3 Scene 1
Viola/Cesario encounters Feste and the two knights; Olivia declares her love for Orsino's messenger.

0s.d. *tabor*: small drum; pipe and tabor were traditional instruments of the stage clown.

1 *Save*: God save.
  live by: earn a living with.
4 *churchman*: priest.
5 *by*: near.
7 *lies by*: a) lies near; b) lies with.
8 *stands by*: is maintained by.
10 *You have said*: just as you say.
   To . . . age: what an age we live in.
10–11 *A sentence . . . wit*: a wise saying is like a soft glove to a clever man.
11 *chev'ril*: kidskin, a soft pliable leather.
13 *dally nicely*: play curiously.
14 *wanton*: wayward, disorderly.
15 *I . . . name*: that's why I wish my sister had no name.
18–19 *words . . . them*: words have become very untrustworthy now that verbal promises ('bonds') cannot be relied on.

SCENE 1

Olivia'*s garden: enter* Viola, *and* Feste, *who plays on his pipe and tabor*

Viola
Save thee, friend, and thy music! Dost thou live by thy tabor?

Feste
No, sir, I live by the church.

Viola
Art thou a churchman?

Feste
5 No such matter, sir. I do live by the church, for I do live at my house, and my house doth stand by the church.

Viola
So thou mayst say the king lies by a beggar, if a beggar dwell near him; or the church stands by thy tabor, if thy tabor stand by the church.

Feste
10 You have said, sir. To see this age! A sentence is but a chev'ril glove to a good wit—how quickly the wrong side may be turned outward!

Viola
Nay, that's certain: they that dally nicely with words may quickly make them wanton.

Feste
15 I would therefore my sister had had no name, sir.

Viola
Why, man?

Feste
Why, sir, her name's a word, and to dally with that word might make my sister wanton. But indeed, words are very rascals, since bonds disgraced them.

Viola
20 Thy reason, man?

Feste
Troth, sir, I can yield you none without words, and
words are grown so false, I am loath to prove reason
with them.
  Viola
  I warrant thou art a merry fellow, and car'st for
25 nothing.
  Feste
Not so, sir, I do care for something; but in my
conscience, sir, I do not care for you: if that be to care
for nothing, sir, I would it would make you invisible.
  Viola
Art not thou the Lady Olivia's fool?
  Feste
30 No indeed sir, the Lady Olivia has no folly. She will keep
no fool, sir, till she be married, and fools are as like
husbands as pilchards are to herrings: the husband's the
bigger. I am indeed not her fool, but her corrupter of
words.
  Viola
35 I saw thee late at the Count Orsino's.
  Feste
Foolery, sir, does walk about the orb like the sun: it
shines everywhere. I would be sorry, sir, but the fool
should be as oft with your master as with my mistress. I
think I saw your wisdom there.
  Viola
40 Nay, an' thou pass upon me, I'll no more with thee.
Hold, there's expenses for thee.

  Gives him a coin

  Feste
Now Jove, in his next commodity of hair, send thee a
beard!
  Viola
By my troth, I'll tell thee, I am almost sick for one—
45 [*Aside*] though I would not have it grow on my chin. Is
thy lady within?
  Feste
Would not a pair of these have bred, sir?

48 *put to use*: invested.

49–50 *Lord . . . Troilus*: Pandarus
introduced his niece Cressida to
Troilus during the Trojan War; the story
is the subject of Shakespeare's play
Troilus and Cressida, and of poems by
Chaucer and Henryson.

52–3 *begging . . . a beggar*: I was only
asking for a beggar because that's
what Cressida was; in Henryson's *The
Testament of Cresseid* the heroine
becomes a leper and is forced to beg
for her living.
54 *conster*: construe, explain.
55 *welkin*: sky.
56 *element*: sky.
overworn: over-used, stale.
58 *craves*: requires.
59 *their . . . jests*: the mood of the people
he is clowning for.
60 *quality*: social status.
time: occasion.
61 *like . . . feather*: like the wild hawk,
swoop down on every prey (i.e. neglect
no opportunity for jesting).
62 *practice*: skill.
63 *art*: profession.
64 *fit*: appropriate.
65 *folly-fall'n*: having fallen to folly.
quite taint: completely spoil.

68 *Dieu . . . monsieur*: God keep you, sir;
Sir Andrew remembers a little French.

69 *Et . . . serviteur*: and you too: at your
service.

Viola
Yes, being kept together, and put to use.
Feste
I would play Lord Pandarus of Phrygia, sir, to bring a
50 Cressida to this Troilus.
Viola
I understand you, sir, 'tis well begged.

Gives him another coin

Feste
The matter, I hope, is not great, sir, begging but a
beggar: Cressida was a beggar. My lady is within, sir. I
will conster to them whence you come; who you are and
55 what you would are out of my welkin—I might say
'element', but the word is overworn.   [*Exit*
Viola
This fellow is wise enough to play the fool,
And to do that well, craves a kind of wit:
He must observe their mood on whom he jests,
60 The quality of persons, and the time,
And, like the haggard, check at every feather
That comes before his eye. This is a practice
As full of labour as a wise man's art:
For folly that he wisely shows is fit;
65 But wise men, folly-fall'n, quite taint their wit.

Enter Sir Toby *and* Sir Andrew

Sir Toby
Save you, gentleman.
Viola
And you, sir.
Sir Andrew
Dieu vous garde, monsieur.
Viola
Et vous aussi: votre serviteur.
Sir Andrew
70 I hope, sir, you are, and I am yours.

71 *encounter*: go to meet.

72 *trade*: business.

73 *bound to*: going towards.
list: limit, destination.

75 *Taste*: try.

76 *understand me*: stand under me.

78 *to go*: to walk.

79 *answer*: obey.
with . . . entrance: by walking inside (with a pun on 'gate').
80 *prevented*: forestalled.

84 *My matter*: what I have to say.
hath no voice: cannot be spoken.
85 *pregnant*: receptive.
vouchsafed: attentive.
86–7 *get . . . ready*: keep them all in mind; perhaps he writes in a notebook.

89 *hearing*: audience, meeting.

Sir Toby
Will you encounter the house? My niece is desirous you should enter, if your trade be to her.
   Viola
I am bound to your niece, sir; I mean, she is the list of my voyage.
   Sir Toby
75 Taste your legs, sir, put them to motion.
   Viola
My legs do better understand me, sir, than I understand what you mean by bidding me taste my legs.
   Sir Toby
I mean, to go, sir, to enter.
   Viola
I will answer you with gait and entrance; but we are
80 prevented.

   Enter Olivia *and* Maria

Most excellent accomplished lady, the heavens rain odours on you!
   Sir Andrew
That youth's a rare courtier: 'rain odours'—well!
   Viola
My matter hath no voice, lady, but to your own most
85 pregnant and vouchsafed ear.
   Sir Andrew
'Odours', 'pregnant', and 'vouchsafed': I'll get 'em all three all ready.
   Olivia
Let the garden door be shut, and leave me to my hearing.   [*Exeunt* Sir Toby, Sir Andrew, *and* Maria
90 Give me your hand, sir.
   Viola
My duty, madam, and most humble service.
   Olivia
What is your name?
   Viola
Cesario is your servant's name, fair princess.

94 *'Twas . . . world*: the world has not been a happy place.
95 *lowly . . . compliment*: fake humility was called flattery.

97 *he . . . be yours*: he is your servant, and what he owns must necessarily be yours.

99 *For*: as for.
on: about.
100 *Would they were blanks*: I would rather they were empty.
101 *whet*: sharpen, excite.

105 *solicit*: argue about.
106 *music . . . spheres*: heavenly harmony (made by the rotation of the planets in their orbits).

107 *Give . . . you*: please let me speak.
108 *After . . . here*: after you had bewitched me last time you were here.
109 *abuse*: deceive, insult.

111 *hard construction*: severe judgement.
112 *that*: i.e. the ring.
113 *none of yours*: was not yours.

114–16 *Have . . . think*: Olivia pictures herself as a bear tied to the stake (see picture p.40) and tormented by all the unrestrained thoughts that a cruel heart can devise.
116 *receiving*: understanding.
117 *a cypress*: a transparent veil.

119 *degree*: step; 'grize' in the next line has the same meaning.

Olivia
My servant, sir? 'Twas never merry world
95 Since lowly feigning was call'd compliment:
Y'are servant to the Count Orsino, youth.
Viola
And he is yours, and his must needs be yours:
Your servant's servant is your servant, madam.
Olivia
For him, I think not on him; for his thoughts,
100 Would they were blanks, rather than fill'd with me.
Viola
Madam, I come to whet your gentle thoughts
On his behalf.
Olivia
     O, by your leave, I pray you!
I bade you never speak again of him;
But would you undertake another suit,
105 I had rather hear you to solicit that,
Than music from the spheres.
Viola
        Dear lady—
Olivia
Give me leave, beseech you. I did send,
After the last enchantment you did here,
A ring in chase of you. So did I abuse
110 Myself, my servant, and, I fear me, you.
Under your hard construction must I sit,
To force that on you in a shameful cunning
Which you knew none of yours. What might you
  think?
Have you not set mine honour at the stake,
115 And baited it with all th' unmuzzled thoughts
That tyrannous heart can think? To one of your
  receiving
Enough is shown; a cypress, not a bosom,
Hides my heart. So, let me hear you speak.
Viola
I pity you.
Olivia
    That's a degree to love.

120 *vulgar proof*: common experience.

122 *'tis . . . again*: I can smile again (because her enemy shows pity).
123 *how . . . proud*: the deprived are so quick to think well of themselves (Olivia is ironic).
126 *upbraids*: reproaches.

128 *is . . . harvest*: has ripened to maturity.
129 *like*: likely.
proper: handsome.
130 *westward ho*: the cry of Thames boatmen for passengers going towards Westminster.
131 *Grace . . . disposition*: the blessing of heaven and peace of mind.
132 *You'll nothing*: you have no message.

135 *you do . . . are*: a) you forget that you are a noblewoman; b) you do not imagine you are in love with a woman.
136 *the . . . you*: i.e. that you are not what you appear to be.
138 *I would . . . be*: I wish you were what I want you to be (i.e. Olivia's lover).
140 *I am your fool*: you're making a fool of me.
141–2 *what . . . lip*: how beautiful he looks with his lips showing angry contempt.
143 *A . . . guilt*: the guilt of a murderer.
144 *love . . . hid*: love that tries to hide itself.
Love . . . noon: the most secret love is as clear as midday.
146 *maidhood*: virginity.
147 *maugre . . . pride*: despite all your unkindness.
148 *Nor . . . reason*: neither intelligence nor sense.
149–50 *Do not . . . cause*: don't force yourself to deduce from this argument ('clause') that because ('For that') I am courting you, there is no need for you to court me.

Viola

120 No, not a grize: for 'tis a vulgar proof
That very oft we pity enemies.
Olivia
Why then methinks 'tis time to smile again.
O world, how apt the poor are to be proud!
If one should be a prey, how much the better
125 To fall before the lion than the wolf! [*Clock strikes*]
The clock upbraids me with the waste of time.
Be not afraid, good youth, I will not have you.
And yet when wit and youth is come to harvest
Your wife is like to reap a proper man.
130 There lies your way, due west.
Viola
                                        Then westward ho!
Grace and good disposition attend your ladyship.
You'll nothing, madam, to my lord by me?
Olivia
Stay!
I prithee, tell me what thou think'st of me.
Viola
135 That you do think you are not what you are.
Olivia
If I think so, I think the same of you.
Viola
Then think you right; I am not what I am.
Olivia
I would you were as I would have you be.
Viola
Would it be better, madam, than I am?
140 I wish it might, for now I am your fool.
Olivia
[*Aside*] O what a deal of scorn looks beautiful
In the contempt and anger of his lip!
A murd'rous guilt shows not itself more soon
Than love that would seem hid. Love's night is noon.
145 Cesario, by the roses of the spring,
By maidhood, honour, truth, and everything,
I love thee so that, maugre all thy pride,
Nor wit nor reason can my passion hide.
Do not extort thy reasons from this clause.

151 *reason . . . fetter*: join one reason to
another like this.

150 For that I woo, thou therefore hast no cause;
But rather reason thus with reason fetter:
Love sought is good, but given unsought is better.
    Viola
By innocence I swear, and by my youth,
I have one heart, one bosom, and one truth,

155 *nor never none*: and there will never
be any woman.

155 And that no woman has; nor never none
Shall mistress be of it, save I alone.
And so adieu, good madam; never more

158 *deplore*: weep out.

Will I my master's tears to you deplore.
    Olivia

159 *move*: persuade.

Yet come again: for thou perhaps mayst move
160 That heart which now abhors, to like his love.

                  [*Exeunt*

Act 3 Scene 2
Sir Andrew's suspicions have been aroused
and he threatens to go home, but Sir Toby
coaxes him to challenge Viola/Cesario to a
duel.

SCENE 2

Olivia'*s house: enter* Sir Toby, Sir Andrew, *and*
Fabian

1 *jot*: moment.

    Sir Andrew
No, faith, I'll not stay a jot longer.
    Sir Toby

2 *dear venom*: sweet poison.

Thy reason, dear venom, give thy reason.
    Fabian

3 *yield*: give.

You must needs yield your reason, Sir Andrew.
    Sir Andrew

4 *Marry*: indeed.

Marry, I saw your niece do more favours to the Count's
5 serving-man than ever she bestowed upon me. I saw't
i' th' orchard.
    Sir Toby

7 *the while*: at the time.

Did she see thee the while, old boy, tell me that?
    Sir Andrew
As plain as I see you now.
    Fabian

9 *argument*: proof.

This was a great argument of love in her toward you.
    Sir Andrew

10 *'Slight*: by God's light.

10 'Slight! Will you make an ass o' me?
    Fabian

11 *legitimate*: logically admissible.
oaths: sworn testimony; Fabian and
Sir Toby try to confuse Sir Andrew.

I will prove it legitimate, sir, upon the oaths of
judgment and reason.

13 *grand-jurymen*: The grand-jury decided whether a case deserved a proper trial.

13–14 *before . . . sailor*: before the Flood.

16 *dormouse*: a very small mouse which sleeps all winter.

18 *accosted*: approached (see *1*, *3*, 45note).

19 *fire-new . . . mint*: as brilliant as newly-minted coins.
banged: beaten.

20–1 *looked . . . hand*: expected from you.

21 *balked*: refused.
double gilt: gilt-plate twice washed with gold.

24 *hang . . . beard*: Fabian alludes to the Dutchman William Barents, who made a famous arctic voyage in 1596–7.

25 *laudable attempt*: special effort.

26 *valour or policy*: bravery or cunning.

27 *An't*: if it.
policy I hate: I hate intrigue.

28 *I had as lief*: I would as willingly.
Brownist: a Puritan sect (founded by Robert Browne in the 16th century).

29 *build me*: go and build; 'me' is used merely for emphasis.

30 *to fight*: by offering to fight.

31 *take note*: notice.

32 *love-broker*: marriage-broker.

37 *curst*: fierce.

39 *invention*: untruth.

39–40 *If thou . . . amiss*: it wouldn't be a bad idea to address him about three times as 'thou' (a form used only to intimates and inferiors).

41 *lies*: falsehoods.

42 *bed of Ware*: a famous carved bed about 3 metres square in Ware, Hertfordshire (now in the Victoria and Albert Museum, London).

43 *set 'em down*: write them down.
about it: get on with it.
gall: a) venom; b) a growth on oak-trees used in making ink.

44 *goose-pen*: pen made from the quill of a goose (proverbially a foolish bird).

Sir Toby

And they have been grand-jurymen since before Noah was a sailor.

Fabian

15 She did show favour to the youth in your sight only to exasperate you, to awake your dormouse valour, to put fire in your heart, and brimstone in your liver. You should then have accosted her, and with some excellent jests, fire-new from the mint, you should have banged

20 the youth into dumbness. This was looked for at your hand, and this was balked. The double gilt of this opportunity you let time wash off, and you are now sailed into the north of my lady's opinion, where you will hang like an icicle on a Dutchman's beard, unless

25 you do redeem it by some laudable attempt, either of valour or policy.

Sir Andrew

An't be any way, it must be with valour, for policy I hate: I had as lief be a Brownist as a politician.

Sir Toby

Why then, build me thy fortunes upon the basis of

30 valour. Challenge me the Count's youth to fight with him; hurt him in eleven places: my niece shall take note of it; and assure thyself there is no love-broker in the world can more prevail in man's commendation with woman than report of valour.

Fabian

35 There is no way but this, Sir Andrew.

Sir Andrew

Will either of you bear me a challenge to him?

Sir Toby

Go, write it in a martial hand. Be curst and brief: it is no matter how witty, so it be eloquent and full of invention. Taunt him with the licence of ink. If thou

40 thou'st him some thrice, it shall not be amiss; and as many lies as will lie in thy sheet of paper, although the sheet were big enough for the bed of Ware in England, set 'em down. Go, about it. Let there be gall enough in thy ink, though thou write with a goose-pen, no matter.

45 About it!

Sir Andrew

Where shall I find you?

Sir Toby

We'll call thee at thy cubiculo. Go! [*Exit* Sir Andrew

Fabian

This is a dear manikin to you, Sir Toby.

Sir Toby

I have been dear to him, lad, some two thousand strong,
50 or so.

Fabian

We shall have a rare letter from him—but you'll not
deliver't—

Sir Toby

Never trust me then? and by all means stir on the youth
to an answer. I think oxen and wainropes cannot hale
55 them together. For Andrew, if he were opened and you
find so much blood in his liver as will clog the foot of a
flea, I'll eat the rest of th' anatomy.

Fabian

And his opposite, the youth, bears in his visage no great
presage of cruelty.

Enter Maria

Sir Toby

60 Look where the youngest wren of nine comes.

Maria

If you desire the spleen, and will laugh yourselves into
stitches, follow me. Yond gull Malvolio is turned
heathen, a very renegado; for there is no Christian, that
means to be saved by believing rightly, can ever believe
65 such impossible passages of grossness. He's in yellow
stockings!

Sir Toby

And cross-gartered?

Maria

Most villainous: like a pedant that keeps a school i' th'
church. I have dogged him like his murderer. He does
70 obey every point of the letter that I dropped to betray

47 *cubiculo*: bed-chamber.

48 *dear manikin*: precious plaything; Sir
Toby plays on 'dear' = expensive.

49 *some . . . strong*: a good two thousand
(ducats).

51 *rare*: extraordinary.

53 *by . . . stir on*: do everything I can to
provoke.
54 *wainropes*: cart-ropes.
hale: drag.
55 *opened*: dissected.
56 *blood . . . liver*: A bloodless liver was
thought to be a sign of cowardice.
57 *anatomy*: corpse.
58 *opposite*: opponent.
visage: face.
59 *presage*: promise.

60 *wren*: a tiny brown bird; the last chick
to hatch is always the smallest.

61 *spleen*: a fit of laughter (thought to
arise from the spleen).
62 *Yond gull*: that idiot.
63 *renegado*: heretic.
64 *means . . . rightly*: hopes for salvation
through orthodox Christian faith.
65 *impossible . . . grossness*: grossly
incredible statements.

68–9 *like . . . church*: like an old-
fashioned schoolmaster who teaches
his class in the church.
69 *dogged him*: followed him closely.

71–2 *more lines . . . Indies*: a new map,
published 1599, showed more details
of the Indies than earlier maps, and
included a network of 'rhumb' lines of
navigation.

him. He does smile his face into more lines than is in the
new map with the augmentation of the Indies: you have
not seen such a thing as 'tis! I can hardly forbear hurling
things at him—I know my lady will strike him. If she
75 do, he'll smile, and take't for a great favour.

Sir Toby

Come bring us, bring us where he is.   [*Exeunt*

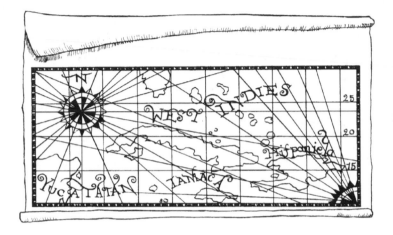

Act 3 Scene 3
Antonio dare not accompany Sebastian on
his sight-seeing tour of Orsino's city, but
insists on lending him some money.

1 *by my will*: willingly.
2 *you make . . . pains*: you enjoy taking
this trouble.
3 *chide*: scold.

4 *stay behind you*: let you go without
me.
5 *filed steel*: filèd; the sharp point of a
steel spur.
6 *not all*: it was not only.
6–7 *so much . . . voyage*: enough love to
make me undertake a longer journey.
8 *jealousy*: anxiety.
9 *skilless in*: a stranger in.
9–11 *to a stranger . . . unhospitable*:
Antonio's view of Illyria is in marked
contrast to the impression created by
the two noble households.
12 *The rather*: even more readily.
13 *in your pursuit*: to follow you.

SCENE 3

The street: enter Sebastian *and* Antonio

Sebastian

I would not by my will have troubled you,
But since you make your pleasure of your pains,
I will no further chide you.

Antonio

I could not stay behind you. My desire,
5 More sharp than filed steel, did spur me forth:
And not all love to see you (though so much
As might have drawn one to a longer voyage)
But jealousy what might befall your travel,
Being skilless in these parts: which to a stranger,
10 Unguided and unfriended, often prove
Rough and unhospitable. My willing love
The rather by these arguments of fear
Set forth in your pursuit.

Sebastian

My kind Antonio,
I can no other answer make, but thanks,
15 And thanks, and ever thanks; and oft good turns
Are shuffled off with such uncurrent pay:
But were my worth, as is my conscience, firm,
You should find better dealing. What's to do?
Shall we go see the relics of this town?

Antonio

20 Tomorrow, sir; best first go see your lodging.

Sebastian

I am not weary, and 'tis long to night.
I pray you, let us satisfy our eyes
With the memorials and the things of fame
That do renown this city.

Antonio

Would you'd pardon me:
25 I do not without danger walk these streets.
Once in a sea-fight 'gainst the Count his galleys,
I did some service—of such note indeed,
That were I ta'en here it would scarce be answer'd.

Sebastian

Belike you slew great number of his people.

Antonio

30 Th' offence is not of such a bloody nature,
Albeit the quality of the time and quarrel
Might well have given us bloody argument.
It might have since been answer'd in repaying
What we took from them, which for traffic's sake
35 Most of our city did. Only myself stood out,
For which, if I be lapsed in this place,
I shall pay dear.

Sebastian

Do not then walk too open.

Antonio

It doth not fit me. Hold, sir, here's my purse.
In the south suburbs, at the Elephant,
40 Is best to lodge. I will bespeak our diet
Whiles you beguile the time, and feed your knowledge
With viewing of the town. There shall you have me.

---

15 *good turns*: kindnesses.
16 *shuffled off*: passed over.
uncurrent pay: valueless repayment.
17 *were . . . firm*: if my wealth were as great as my sense of being indebted.
18 *dealing*: treatment.
What's to do: what shall we do.
19 *relics*: sights, antiquities.

21 *'tis long to night*: there's a long time before nightfall.

24 *renown*: make famous.
Would . . . me: you'll have to excuse me.

26 *the Count his*: the Count's.
27 *service*: fighting.
of such note: so considerable.
28 *ta'en*: arrested.
scarce be answer'd: be hard to account for.
29 *Belike*: I suppose.

31–2 *Albeit . . . argument*: although the nature of the occasion and the dispute might well have given us cause for bloodshed.
33–4 *It might . . . them*: perhaps the quarrel has since been settled by repaying what we took from them.
34 *traffic's sake*: the sake of trading.
35 *stood out*: refused to pay.
36 *lapsed*: lapsèd; apprehended.

37 *open*: conspicuously.

38 *It . . . me*: I don't intend to.
39 *Elephant*: the name of an inn (spelled 'Oliphant') near Shakespeare's Bankside theatre.
40 *bespeak our diet*: order our meals.
41 *beguile the time*: amuse yourself.
42 *have me*: find me.

43 *Why I your purse?*: Why should I take
   your money.

44 *Haply*: perhaps.
   some toy: some little thing.
45–6 *your store . . . markets*: I don't
   think your own money ('store') is
   enough for casual purchases.

47 *purse-bearer*: treasurer.

Sebastian
Why I your purse?
Antonio
Haply your eye shall light upon some toy
45 You have desire to purchase: and your store,
I think, is not for idle markets, sir.
Sebastian
I'll be your purse-bearer, and leave you for
An hour.
Antonio
           To th' Elephant.
Sebastian
                             I do remember.
                        [*Exeunt separately*

Act 3 Scene 4
Olivia, puzzled by his strange behaviour,
puts Malvolio into the care of Sir Toby—
who is making sure that his two duellists
are terrified of each other. But Antonio
rescues Viola (mistaking her for Sebastian),
and is himself arrested.

1 *he says*: if he says (Olivia visualizes a
   possible situation).
2 *of*: on.
3 *youth*: young men; Olivia cynically
   adapts the proverb 'better to buy than
   to borrow'.
5 *sad and civil*: sober and serious.

9 *possessed*: taken over by the devil,
   mad.

12 *were best*: would be advised.

Scene 4

Olivia's garden: enter Olivia *and* Maria

Olivia
[*Aside*] I have sent after him, he says he'll come:
How shall I feast him? What bestow of him?
For youth is bought more oft than begg'd or borrow'd.
I speak too loud.—
5 Where's Malvolio? He is sad and civil,
And suits well for a servant with my fortunes:
Where is Malvolio?
Maria
He's coming, madam, but in very strange manner. He is
sure possessed, madam.
Olivia
10 Why, what's the matter? Does he rave?ˈ
Maria
No, madam, he does nothing but smile: your ladyship
were best to have some guard about you if he come, for
sure the man is tainted in's wits.
Olivia
Go call him hither. [*Exit* Maria] I am as mad as he
15 If sad and merry madness equal be.

18 *upon a sad occasion*: about a serious matter.

22 *sonnet*: song: Malvolio quotes the first line of a popular ballad.
23 *how dost thou*: how are you.
25 *Not . . . mind*: not melancholy.
though . . . legs: although my legs are yellow (a colour associated with melancholy).
25–6 *It did . . . hands*: the letter reached the right man's hands.
27–8 *the sweet Roman hand*: the elegant italic script (more fashionable at this time than the ordinary English handwriting).

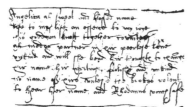

Elizabethan English script

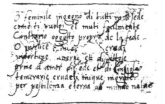

Italian style of handwriting

29 *Ay, sweetheart . . . thee*: a line from a popular song.
33 *At your request*: must I answer someone like you; Malvolio is obeying the injunction to be 'surly with servants' (*2, 5, 138*).
daws: jackdaws.

Enter Malvolio *with* Maria

How now, Malvolio?
Malvolio
Sweet Lady, ho, ho!
Olivia
Smil'st thou? I sent for thee upon a sad occasion.
Malvolio
Sad, lady? I could be sad: this does make some
20 obstruction in the blood, this cross-gartering; but what of that? If it please the eye of one, it is with me as the very true sonnet is: '*Please one, and please all*'.
Olivia
Why, how dost thou, man? What is the matter with thee?
Malvolio
25 Not black in my mind, though yellow in my legs. It did come to his hands, and commands shall be executed. I think we do know the sweet Roman hand.
Olivia
Wilt thou go to bed, Malvolio?
Malvolio
To bed? *Ay, sweetheart, and I'll come to thee.*
Olivia
30 God comfort thee! Why dost thou smile so, and kiss thy hand so oft?
Maria
How do you, Malvolio?
Malvolio
At your request? Yes, nightingales answer daws!
Maria
Why appear you with this ridiculous boldness before
35 my lady?
Malvolio
'Be not afraid of greatness': 'twas well writ.
Olivia
What mean'st thou by that, Malvolio?
Malvolio
'Some are born great—'
Olivia
Ha?

Malvolio

40 'Some achieve greatness—'

Olivia

What say'st thou?

Malvolio

'And some have greatness thrust upon them.'

Olivia

Heaven restore thee!

Malvolio

'Remember who commended thy yellow stockings—'

Olivia

45 Thy yellow stockings?

Malvolio

'And wished to see thee cross-gartered.'

Olivia

Cross-gartered?

Malvolio

'Go to, thou art made, if thou desir'st to be so—'

Olivia

Am I made?

Malvolio

50 'If not, let me see thee a servant still.'

Olivia

Why, this is very midsummer madness.

Enter Servant

Servant

Madam, the young gentleman of the Count Orsino's is returned; I could hardly entreat him back. He attends your ladyship's pleasure.

Olivia

55 I'll come to him. [*Exit* Servant] Good Maria, let this fellow be looked to. Where's my cousin Toby? Let some of my people have a special care of him; I would not have him miscarry for the half of my dowry.

[*Exeunt* Olivia *and* Maria *different ways*

Malvolio

O ho, do you come near me now? No worse man than

60 Sir Toby to look to me! This concurs directly with the

48 *thou art made*: your fortune is made—but Olivia thinks Malvolio is saying that she is 'mad'.

51 *very . . . madness*: a real fit of lunacy; the phrase was proverbial.

53 *I . . . back*: I could hardly restrain him.

58 *miscarry*: come to harm.

59 *come near*: begin to understand.

60 *to look to*: to take care of.
concurs: agrees.

62 *stubborn*: rude.

66 *consequently*: accordingly.
sets down: describes.
67 *sad*: serious.
reverend carriage: dignified
deportment.
67–8 *in . . . note*: in the style of some
important personage.
68–9 *limed her*: caught her (like a bird
on a branch sticky with lime).
71 *Fellow*: Malvolio persuades himself
that Olivia is referring to him as her
equal.
degree: rank (as steward).
72 *adheres*: accords.
72–3 *no dram . . . scruple*: not the tiniest
little amount; 'dram' and 'scruple' are
apothecary's weights.
72 *dram*: ⅛ ounce (1 ounce = 28 grams).
73 *scruple*: a) ⅓ dram; b) doubt.
74 *incredulous*: incredible.
76 *full . . . hopes*: fulfilment of all my
hopes.
78 *sanctity*: Sir Toby invokes divine
protection before tackling the
supposed devil possessing Malvolio.
79 *drawn in little*: a) portrayed in
miniature; b) contracted into one
body.
Legion: the name claimed by the devil
possessing a madman in St Mark's
Gospel (5:8–9).
83 *discard*: reject.
private: privacy.

84 *hollow*: a) deceptively; b) spookily.

89 *Let me alone*: leave me to handle him
alone.
90 *defy*: renounce.

letter: she sends him on purpose, that I may appear
stubborn to him; for she incites me to that in the letter.
'Cast thy humble slough,' says she; 'be opposite with a
kinsman, surly with servants, let thy tongue tang
65 arguments of state, put thyself into the trick of
singularity'—and consequently sets down the manner
how: as, a sad face, a reverend carriage, a slow tongue, in
the habit of some sir of note, and so forth. I have limed
her, but it is Jove's doing, and Jove make me thankful!
70 And when she went away now, 'Let this fellow be looked
to'. 'Fellow'! Not Malvolio, nor after my degree, but
'fellow'. Why, everything adheres together, that no dram
of a scruple, no scruple of a scruple, no obstacle, no
incredulous or unsafe circumstance—what can be
75 said?—nothing that can be can come between me and
the full prospect of my hopes. Well, Jove, not I, is the
doer of this, and he is to be thanked.

Enter Sir Toby, Fabian, *and* Maria

Sir Toby
Which way is he, in the name of sanctity? If all the devils
of hell be drawn in little, and Legion himself possessed
80 him, yet I'll speak to him.
Fabian
Here he is, here he is. How is't with you, sir? How is't
with you, man?
Malvolio
Go off, I discard you. Let me enjoy my private. Go off.
Maria
Lo, how hollow the fiend speaks within him! Did not I
85 tell you? Sir Toby, my lady prays you to have a care of
him.
Malvolio
[*Aside*] Ah ha! Does she so?
Sir Toby
Go to, go to: peace, peace, we must deal gently with him.
Let me alone. How do you, Malvolio? How is't with you?
90 What, man, defy the devil! Consider, he's an enemy to
mankind.

95　*Carry his water*: take a urine
specimen.
　wise woman: i.e. a 'good' witch,
skilled in occult arts and sciences.
96　*if I live*: as sure as I'm alive.

101　*move*: excite.

102　*rough*: violent.

104–6　*bawcock . . . chuck . . . biddy*: fine
fellow . . . chicken . . . chickabiddy
(terms of endearment spoken to
children).

106–7　*'tis not . . . Satan*: it's not right for
a sensible man ('gravity') to be playing
children's games with the devil.
107　*cherry-pit*: a game of throwing cherry-
stones into a hole.
　foul collier: dirty coalman
(traditionally said to be black in heart
as well as in appearance).
110　*minx*: shameless woman.

112–13　*I am . . . element*: I am out of
your sphere, I am superior to you.
113　*hereafter*: later.

Malvolio

Do you know what you say?

Maria

La you, an' you speak ill of the devil, how he takes it at
heart! Pray God he be not bewitched!

Fabian

95　Carry his water to th' wise woman.

Maria

Marry, and it shall be done tomorrow morning, if I live.
My lady would not lose him for more than I'll say.

Malvolio

How now, mistress?

Maria

O Lord!

Sir Toby

100　Prithee hold thy peace, this is not the way. Do you not
see you move him? Let me alone with him.

Fabian

No way but gentleness, gently, gently: the fiend is rough,
and will not be roughly used.

Sir Toby

Why, how now, my bawcock? How dost thou, chuck?

Malvolio

105　Sir!

Sir Toby

Ay, biddy, come with me. What, man, 'tis not for gravity
to play at cherry-pit with Satan. Hang him, foul collier!

Maria

Get him to say his prayers, good Sir Toby, get him to
pray.

Malvolio

110　My prayers, minx!

Maria

No, I warrant you, he will not hear of godliness.

Malvolio

Go hang yourselves all. You are idle, shallow things; I
am not of your element. You shall know more hereafter.

[*Exit*

115–16 *If this . . . fiction*: Shakespeare draws attention to the unreality of theatrical illusion.
115 *played*: performed.
could: would.
116 *an improbable fiction*: something that could never happen.
117 *genius*: nature, guiding spirit.
taken: caught.
device: plot.
119 *take air*: becomes known, comes into the open.
taint: gets spoiled.

122 *we'll . . . bound*: This was standard treatment of the insane.
123–4 *carry it thus*: keep this up.

125 *pastime*: amusement.
126–7 *bring . . . bar*: let our trick be brought to the bar for public judgement.
127 *finder*: judge, one who can identify.

129 *matter . . . morning*: games for a holiday (especially the morris-games of May Day).
130–1 *vinegar and pepper in't*: it is highly spiced (= insolent).

132 *saucy*: cheeky—with a play on 'vinegar and pepper'.

133 *I warrant him*: I can assure you.

134 *whatsoever*: of whatever degree.
thou: Sir Andrew uses the familiar form—in accordance with Sir Toby's advice (*3, 2, 39–40*).

Sir Toby
Is't possible?
Fabian
115 If this were played upon a stage now, I could condemn it as an improbable fiction.
Sir Toby
His very genius hath taken the infection of the device, man.
Maria
Nay, pursue him now, lest the device take air, and taint.
Fabian
120 Why, we shall make him mad indeed.
Maria
The house will be the quieter.
Sir Toby
Come, we'll have him in a dark room and bound. My niece is already in the belief that he's mad: we may carry it thus for our pleasure, and his penance, till our very
125 pastime, tired out of breath, prompt us to have mercy on him; at which time we will bring the device to the bar, and crown thee for a finder of madmen. But see, but see!

Enter Sir Andrew

Fabian
More matter for a May morning!
Sir Andrew
130 Here's the challenge, read it: I warrant there's vinegar and pepper in't.
Fabian
Is't so saucy?
Sir Andrew
Ay, is't, I warrant him: do but read.
Sir Toby
Give me. [*Reads*] *Youth, whatsoever thou art, thou art*
135 *but a scurvy fellow.*
Fabian
Good and valiant.

137 *admire not*: do not marvel.

139 *keeps . . . law*: protects you from legal action; Sir Andrew's gibes are surprisingly careful in their phrasing.
140 *uses*: treats.
141 *thou . . . throat*: you are a complete liar (see *3, 2, 41*).

143 *sense . . . less*: The 'less' is not intended for Sir Andrew's hearing.

144 *chance*: good luck.

147 *like . . . villain*: The terms could refer equally to 'thou' or to 'me': Sir Andrew maintains his ambiguity.
148 *o'th' windy side*: on the safe side; a seaman sails *with* the wind to avoid being driven on to the rocks.

150 *my . . . better*: I have more hope of beating you.
151 *look to*: take care of.
    as . . . him: if you treat him as a friend.

153 *move*: a) anger; b) propel.

156 *commerce*: conversation.

157 *scout me*: keep a look-out.
158 *bum-baily*: bailiff (who comes up behind the man he is arresting).
    So: as.
159 *draw*: draw your sword.
160 *comes to pass oft*: often happens.
161 *sharply twanged off*: pronounced boldly.
161–2 *gives . . . approbation*: gives a man greater credit for courage.
162 *proof*: being put to the test.
164 *let me alone*: you can't beat me.

Sir Toby

Wonder not, nor admire not in thy mind, why I do call thee so, for I will show thee no reason for't.

Fabian

A good note; that keeps you from the blow of the law.

Sir Toby

140 *Thou com'st to the Lady Olivia, and in my sight she uses thee kindly: but thou liest in thy throat; that is not the matter I challenge thee for.*

Fabian

Very brief, and to exceeding good sense [*Aside*]-less!

Sir Toby

I will waylay thee going home, where if it be thy chance to
145 *kill me—*

Fabian

Good!

Sir Toby

Thou kill'st me like a rogue and a villain.

Fabian

Still you keep o' th' windy side of the law: good.

Sir Toby

Fare thee well, and God have mercy upon one of our souls!
150 *He may have mercy upon mine, but my hope is better, and so look to thyself. Thy friend, as thou usest him, and thy sworn enemy,*

Andrew Aguecheek.

If this letter move him not, his legs cannot. I'll give't him.

Maria

155 You may have very fit occasion for't. He is now in some commerce with my lady, and will by and by depart.

Sir Toby

So, Sir Andrew: scout me for him at the corner of the orchard, like a bum-baily. So soon as ever thou see'st him, draw, and as thou draw'st, swear horrible—for it
160 comes to pass oft that a terrible oath, with a swaggering accent sharply twanged off, gives manhood more approbation than ever proof itself would have earned him. Away!

Sir Andrew

Nay, let me alone for swearing.   [*Exit*

Sir Toby

165 Now will not I deliver his letter. For the behaviour of the young gentleman gives him out to be of good capacity and breeding: his employment between his lord and my niece confirms no less. Therefore this letter, being so excellently ignorant, will breed no terror in the youth:

170 he will find it comes from a clodpole. But sir, I will deliver his challenge by word of mouth, set upon Aguecheek a notable report of valour, and drive the gentleman (as I know his youth will aptly receive it) into a most hideous opinion of his rage, skill, fury, and

175 impetuosity. This will so fright them both that they will kill one another by the look, like cockatrices.

Enter Olivia *and* Viola

Fabian

Here he comes with your niece. Give them way till he take leave, and presently after him.

Sir Toby

I will meditate the while upon some horrid message for

180 a challenge.   [*Exeunt* Sir Toby, Fabian, *and* Maria

Olivia

I have said too much unto a heart of stone,
And laid mine honour too unchary out.
There's something in me that reproves my fault,
But such a headstrong potent fault it is

185 That it but mocks reproof.

Viola

With the same 'haviour that your passion bears
Goes on my master's griefs.

Olivia

Here, wear this jewel for me, 'tis my picture:
Refuse it not, it hath no tongue to vex you.

190 And I beseech you come again tomorrow.
What shall you ask of me that I'll deny,
That honour sav'd may upon asking give?

Viola

Nothing but this: your true love for my master.

Olivia

How with mine honour may I give him that

---

166 *gives him out*: shows him.
166–7 *of good . . . breeding*: very intelligent and well-educated.
167 *his employment*: the way he is employed (as a messenger).
169 *breed*: give rise to.
170 *clodpole*: blockhead.
171–2 *set . . . valour*: tell him that Aguecheek has a remarkable reputation for courage.
173 *aptly receive it*: be quick to understand it.
174 *hideous*: fearful.
176 *cockatrices*: fabulous serpents which could kill their opponents with a single glance.

177 *give them way*: keep out of their way.
178 *and . . . him*: then immediately go after him.
182 *laid . . . out*: risked my reputation unwisely.
186 *'haviour*: behaviour.
188 *my picture*: Olivia's gift of a jewelled miniature recalls the unveiling of her 'picture' in *Act 1*, Scene 5.

191–2 *What . . . give*: you can't ask me for anything that, saving my honour, I wouldn't give you immediately.

195 *acquit you*: release you (from that gift).

197 *like thee*: in your likeness.

200 *That . . . to't*: make use of whatever skill in fencing you have.
201 *thou*: that you.
202 *intercepter*: adversary.
despite: ill will.
bloody . . . hunter: bloodthirsty like a dog hunting its prey.
attends: is lying in wait.
203 *Dismount thy tuck*: unsheathe your rapier.
yare: prompt.
206 *to*: with.
207 *remembrance*: recollection.
208 *image*: memory.

209–10 *if . . . price*: if you value your life at all.

211 *opposite*: opponent.
212 *furnish man withal*: equip a man with.

213 *what is he*: what rank is he.
214 *knight . . . rapier*: dubbed a knight with sword never drawn from its sheathe.
215 *carpet consideration*: for domestic (not military) service—and perhaps for payment.
216 *Souls . . . three*: he has killed three men.
217 *incensement*: rage.
219 *sepulchre*: burial.
Hob, nob: have it or have it not.
give't or take't: kill or be killed.
220–1 *desire . . . lady*: ask the lady to give me an escort.

195 Which I have given to you?
Viola
                                                   I will acquit you.
Olivia
Well, come again tomorrow. Fare thee well;
A fiend like thee might bear my soul to hell.   [*Exit*

Enter Sir Toby *and* Fabian

Sir Toby
Gentleman, God save thee.
Viola
And you, sir.
Sir Toby
200 That defence thou hast, betake thee to't. Of what nature the wrongs are thou hast done him, I know not; but thy intercepter, full of despite, bloody as the hunter, attends thee at the orchard-end. Dismount thy tuck, be yare in thy preparation, for thy assailant is quick, skilful, and
205 deadly.
Viola
You mistake, sir; I am sure no man hath any quarrel to me: my remembrance is very free and clear from any image of offence done to any man.
Sir Toby
You'll find it otherwise, I assure you. Therefore, if you
210 hold your life at any price, betake you to your guard; for your opposite hath in him what youth, strength, skill, and wrath, can furnish man withal.
Viola
I pray you, sir, what is he?
Sir Toby
He is knight dubbed with unhatched rapier, and on
215 carpet consideration, but he is a devil in private brawl. Souls and bodies hath he divorced three, and his incensement at this moment is so implacable that satisfaction can be none but by pangs of death and sepulchre. Hob, nob, is his word: give't or take't.
Viola
220 I will return again into the house, and desire some conduct of the lady. I am no fighter. I have heard of

278 *Give ground*: yield.

Fabian
[*To* Sir Andrew] Give ground if you see him furious.
Sir Toby
Come, Sir Andrew, there's no remedy; the gentleman
280 *one bout*: i.e. one thrust and parry.   280 will for his honour's sake have one bout with you. He
281 *duello*: code of rules governing the   cannot by the duello avoid it, but he has promised me,
conduct of a duel.   as he is a gentleman and a soldier, he will not hurt you.
283 *to't*: get on with it.   Come on, to't.
Sir Andrew
Pray God he keep his oath!

Enter Antonio

Viola
285 I do assure you, 'tis against my will.

Sir Andrew *and* Viola *draw their swords*

Antonio
[*Drawing*] Put up your sword! If this young gentleman
Have done offence, I take the fault on me:
288 *I for . . . you*: challenge you on his   If you offend him, I for him defy you.
behalf.   **Sir Toby**
You, sir? Why, what are you?
Antonio
290 One, sir, that for his love dares yet do more
Than you have heard him brag to you he will.
Sir Toby
292 *undertaker*: one who acts on another's   Nay, if you be an undertaker, I am for you.
behalf.
I am for you: I am ready to fight you.

Draws

292s.d. *Officers*: the state policemen (who   *Enter* Two Officers
presumably come in from the street).
Fabian
O good Sir Toby, hold! Here come the officers.
Sir Toby
[*To* Antonio] I'll be with you anon.
294 *I'll . . . anon*: I'll see you later; Sir   **Viola**
Toby will not fight in the presence of
the Officers.
295 *put . . . up*: put your sword away.   295 [*To* Sir Andrew] Pray sir, put your sword up, if you
please.

297 *Marry, will I*: I most certainly will.
    for that: as for that which.
298 *He*: i.e. 'grey Capilet'.
    reins well: goes well in a bridle.
299 *office*: duty.

300 *at the suit*: on the authority.

302 *favour*: face.

306 *answer it*: a) atone for it by repayment
    (see *3, 3, 28,33–4*); b) make a
    defence for myself.

310 *befalls myself*: happens to me.
    amaz'd: bewildered.
311 *be of comfort*: cheer up.

313 *entreat of you*: ask you for.

316 *part*: partly.
317 *lean . . . ability*: very little money.
318 *My . . . much*: I do not have much.
319 *I'll . . . present*: I'll divide what I have
    now.
320 *coffer*: wealth.

321 *deny*: refuse.
322 *my deserts to you*: what I deserve from
    you.
323 *lack persuasion*: fail to persuade you.
    tempt: provoke.

Sir Andrew
Marry, will I, sir: and for that I promised you, I'll be as
good as my word. He will bear you easily, and reins well.
First Officer
This is the man; do thy office.
Second Officer
300 Antonio, I arrest thee at the suit
Of Count Orsino.
Antonio
                              You do mistake me, sir.
First Officer
No, sir, no jot: I know your favour well,
Though now you have no sea-cap on your head.
Take him away; he knows I know him well.
Antonio
305 I must obey. [*To* Viola] This comes with seeking you;
But there's no remedy, I shall answer it.
What will you do, now my necessity
Makes me ask you for my purse? It grieves me
Much more for what I cannot do for you,
310 Than what befalls myself. You stand amaz'd,
But be of comfort.
Second Officer
Come, sir, away.
Antonio
I must entreat of you some of that money.
Viola
What money, sir?
315 For the fair kindness you have show'd me here,
And part being prompted by your present trouble,
Out of my lean and low ability
I'll lend you something. My having is not much;
I'll make division of my present with you.
320 Hold, there's half my coffer.

Offers Antonio *money*

Antonio
Will you deny me now? [*Refuses it*]
Is't possible that my deserts to you
Can lack persuasion? Do not tempt my misery,

<table>
<tr><td>324</td><td>unsound: morally weak.</td></tr>
<tr><td>325</td><td>upbraid: reproach.</td></tr>
</table>

324 *unsound*: morally weak.
325 *upbraid*: reproach.

329 *vainness*: boasting.

331 *Inhabits . . . blood*: is inherent in weak human nature.

335 *Reliev'd*: took care.
sanctity of love: pure and intense devotion.
336 *image*: appearance.
336–7 *promise . . . worth*: show itself to be worthy of great respect.
337 *did I devotion*: I worshipped.
340 *done . . . shame*: abused a good appearance.
341–4 *In nature . . . devil*: Antonio suddenly shifts into moralizing rhyming couplets.
342 *unkind*: a) cruel; b) unnatural.
343–4 *the beauteous . . . devil*: beautiful people who are wicked are merely empty bodies, decorated over by the devil.

348 *so do not I*: I do not believe—i.e. that what she has heard is true.

350 *ta'en*: mistaken.

352 *a couplet or two*: Sir Toby derides Antonio's sententious couplets.
sage saws: wise sayings.

Lest that it make me so unsound a man
325 As to upbraid you with those kindnesses
That I have done for you.
    Viola
                        I know of none,
Nor know I you by voice or any feature.
I hate ingratitude more in a man
Than lying, vainness, babbling drunkenness,
330 Or any taint of vice whose strong corruption
Inhabits our frail blood.
    Antonio
                          O heavens themselves!
    Second Officer
Come, sir, I pray you go.
    Antonio
Let me speak a little. This youth that you see here
I snatch'd one half out of the jaws of death,
335 Reliev'd him with such sanctity of love,
And to his image, which methought did promise
Most venerable worth, did I devotion.
    First Officer
What's that to us? The time goes by. Away!
    Antonio
But O how vile an idol proves this god!
340 Thou hast, Sebastian, done good feature shame.
In nature there's no blemish but the mind:
None can be call'd deform'd but the unkind.
Virtue is beauty, but the beauteous evil
Are empty trunks, o'er-flourish'd by the devil.
    First Officer
345 The man grows mad, away with him! Come, come, sir.
    Antonio
Lead me on.   [*Exit with* Officers
    Viola
Methinks his words do from such passion fly
That he believes himself; so do not I!
Prove true, imagination, O prove true,
350 That I, dear brother, be now ta'en for you!
    Sir Toby
Come hither, knight, come hither, Fabian. We'll whisper
o'er a couplet or two of most sage saws.

353–4 *I . . . glass*: I see a living image
of my brother every time I look in
the mirror.
354 *even . . . so*: exactly like this.
355 *favour*: face.
356 *Still . . . fashion*: always in clothes
of this style.

359 *dishonest*: dishonourable.
paltry: contemptible.
360 *a hare*: A proverbial instance of
cowardice.
361 *in necessity*: when he was in need.
denying him: refusing to recognize
him.
cowardship: cowardice.
363 *most . . . in it*: most sincere coward,
devoted to cowardice like a religion.
364 *'Slid*: by God's eyelid.
I'll after: I'll go after.

365 *cuff him soundly*: give him a good
slap with your hand.

366 *An*: if.

367 *the event*: what will happen.

368 *lay any money*: bet any amount of
money.
yet: after all.

Viola
He nam'd Sebastian. I my brother know
Yet living in my glass; even such and so
355 In favour was my brother, and he went
Still in this fashion, colour, ornament,
For him I imitate. O if it prove,
Tempests are kind, and salt waves fresh in love!   [*Exit*
    Sir Toby
A very dishonest paltry boy, and more a coward than a
360 hare. His dishonesty appears in leaving his friend here
in necessity, and denying him; and for his cowardship,
ask Fabian.
    Fabian
A coward, a most devout coward, religious in it!
    Sir Andrew
'Slid, I'll after him again, and beat him.
    Sir Toby
365 Do, cuff him soundly, but never draw thy sword.
    Sir Andrew
An' I do not—   [*Exit*
    Fabian
Come, let's see the event.
    Sir Toby
I dare lay any money 'twill be nothing yet.   [*Exeunt*

ACT 4

Act 4 Scene 1
Feste and Sir Toby mistake Sebastian for his twin, but their attempt to renew the fighting is interrupted by Olivia.

SCENE 1

The street: enter Sebastian *and* Feste

Feste
Will you make me believe that I am not sent for you?
Sebastian
Go to, go to, thou art a foolish fellow, let me be clear of thee.
Feste
Well held out, i' faith! No, I do not know you, nor I am
5 not sent to you by my lady to bid you come speak with her; nor your name is not Master Cesario; nor this is not my nose neither. Nothing that is so, is so.
Sebastian
I prithee vent thy folly somewhere else. Thou know'st not me.
Feste
10 Vent my folly! He has heard that word of some great man, and now applies it to a fool. Vent my folly! I am afraid this great lubber, the world, will prove a cockney. I prithee now, ungird thy strangeness, and tell me what I shall vent to my lady. Shall I vent to her that thou art
15 coming?
Sebastian
I prithee, foolish Greek, depart from me. There's money for thee: if you tarry longer, I shall give worse payment.
Feste
By my troth, thou hast an open hand. These wise men that give fools money get themselves a good report—
20 after fourteen years' purchase.

1 *am not sent*: have not been sent.

2 *Go to*: go away.
   clear: rid.

4 *held out*: sustained; the misunderstanding has been going on for some time.

10 *vent*: get rid of.
   of: spoken by.

12 *lubber*: lout.
   prove: turn out to be.
   cockney: pretentious fop.
13 *ungird thy strangeness*: put off this outlandish behaviour.
14 *vent*: utter.

16 *foolish Greek*: silly clown (a 'merry Greek' = one who talks nonsense).
17 *tarry*: stay around.

18 *open*: generous; Feste remembers earlier gifts (*Act 3*, Scene 1).
19 *report*: reputation.
20 *after . . . purchase*: for a good price; the purchase-price of a piece of land was reckoned to be the sum of twelve or fourteen years' rent.

Enter Sir Andrew, Sir Toby, *and* Fabian

Sir Andrew

21   *There's for you*: take that.

Now, sir, have I met you again? There's for you!

Strikes Sebastian

Sebastian

22   *there's . . . there*: Sebastian probably
     beats Sir Andrew with the hilt of his
     dagger.

Why, there's for thee, and there, and there!

Beats Sir Andrew

24 *Hold*: stop.

25 *straight*: at once.
26 *coats*: places.

28 *go . . . work*: use different tactics.
29 *have . . . battery*: bring a charge of unlawful assault.
30–1 *its . . . that*: that won't matter.

34 *put . . . iron*: sheath your sword.
you . . . fleshed: you are eager for combat.

36 *tempt*: try.

38 *malapert*: impudent.

39 *charge*: command.

41 *Will . . . thus*: is it always going to be like this.

43 *preach'd*: taught.

Are all the people mad?

Sir Toby

Hold, sir, or I'll throw your dagger o'er the house.

Feste

25 This will I tell my lady straight. I would not be in some of your coats for twopence.   [*Exit*

Sir Toby

Come on, sir, hold!

Sir Andrew

Nay, let him alone, I'll go another way to work with him. I'll have an action of battery against him, if there be any
30 law in Illyria; though I struck him first, yet it's no matter for that.

Sebastian

Let go thy hand!

Sir Toby

Come, sir, I will not let you go. Come, my young soldier, put up your iron: you are well fleshed. Come on!

Sebastian

35 I will be free from thee. What would'st thou now? If thou dar'st tempt me further, draw thy sword.

Draws

Sir Toby

What, what! Nay, then, I must have an ounce or two of this malapert blood from you.

Draws

Enter Olivia

Olivia

Hold, Toby! on thy life I charge thee, hold!

Sir Toby

40 Madam!

Olivia

Will it be ever thus? Ungracious wretch,
Fit for the mountains and the barbarous caves
Where manners ne'er were preach'd! Out of my sight!
Be not offended, dear Cesario.

45 *Rudesby*: ruffian.
46 *sway*: rule.
47 *uncivil and unjust*: barbarous and unjustified.
  extent: act of violence.
49 *fruitless*: pointless.
50 *botch'd up*: patched up.
  thereby: because of that.
51 *Thou . . . go*: you must go with me.
52 *deny*: refuse.
  Beshrew: a (mild) curse upon.
53 *He . . . thee*: he stirred up my heart when he attacked you; Olivia alludes to the romantic notion that lovers exchange hearts with each other.
  started: a) startled; b) aroused—leading to a pun on 'heart' and hart'(= deer).
54 *What . . . this*: what does this taste of (i.e. mean).
  How . . . stream: what's going on.
55 *Or . . . or*: either . . . or.
56 *Let . . . steep*: let imagination for ever ('still') drown my reason in the river of forgetfulness.
  Lethe: one of the rivers in the classical underworld whose waters brought total oblivion.
58 *would . . . me*: I wish you would let yourself be guided by me.
59 *say . . . so be*: say you will be so ruled, and be so indeed.

45 Rudesby, be gone!
                    [*Exeunt* Sir Toby, Sir Andrew, *and* Fabian
                              I prithee, gentle friend,
  Let thy fair wisdom, not thy passion, sway
  In this uncivil and unjust extent
  Against thy peace. Go with me to my house,
  And hear thou there how many fruitless pranks
50 This ruffian hath botch'd up, that thou thereby
  May'st smile at this. Thou shalt not choose but go:
  Do not deny. Beshrew his soul for me!
  He started one poor heart of mine, in thee.
      Sebastian
  [*Aside*] What relish is in this? How runs the stream?
55 Or I am mad, or else this is a dream:
  Let fancy still my sense in Lethe steep;
  If it be thus to dream, still let me sleep!
      Olivia
  Nay, come, I prithee; would thou'dst be rul'd by me!
      Sebastian
  Madam, I will.
      Olivia
            O, say so, and so be.   [*Exeunt*

Act 4 Scene 2
Malvolio, locked in a dark room, is being treated like a madman, but Sir Toby is ready to put an end to the joke.

2 *Sir Topas*: The topaz, a precious stone, was believed to control lunatic passions, but Shakespeare probably takes this name from Chaucer's 'Tale of Sir Topas' (*Canterbury Tales*); 'Sir' was a complimentary title for clerics (see *3, 4*, 249).

3 *the whilst*: meanwhile.
4 *dissemble*: disguise.
4–5 *I would*: I wish.
5 *dissembled*: pretended to be something they were not.
6 *tall*: sturdy.
   become . . . well: be really impressive in this role.
7 *student*: scholar (traditionally haggard through much study).
8 *said*: called.
   honest: honourable.
   good housekeeper: hospitable man.
8–9 *goes as fairly*: is just as suitable.
10 *competitors*: confederates.
12–16 *Bonos dies*: good day. In his caricature of a parson, Feste begins with bad Latin (for *bonus dies*), invents the authority of the 'hermit' ('Gorboduc' was a legendary king of England), and develops a mock-logic string of nonsense.
18 *Peace in this prison*: the greeting is prescribed in the Elizabethan *Book of Common Prayer* for the priest's entry into a sickroom.
19 *knave*: lad (used with friendly familiarity of servants).
20s.d. *Within*: offstage.

Scene 2

Olivia's house: enter Maria *and* Feste

Maria
Nay, I prithee put on this gown, and this beard; make him believe thou art Sir Topas the curate. Do it quickly. I'll call Sir Toby the whilst.   [*Exit*
Feste
Well, I'll put it on, and I will dissemble myself in't; and I
5 would I were the first that ever dissembled in such a gown. I am not tall enough to become the function well, nor lean enough to be thought a good student. But to be said an honest man and a good housekeeper goes as fairly as to say a careful man and a great scholar. The
10 competitors enter.

Enter Sir Toby *and* Maria

Sir Toby
Jove bless thee, Master Parson.
Feste
Bonos dies, Sir Toby: for as the old hermit of Prague, that never saw pen and ink, very wittily said to a niece of King Gorboduc, 'That that is, is': so I, being Master
15 Parson, am Master Parson; for what is 'that' but 'that'? and 'is' but 'is'?
Sir Toby
To him, Sir Topas.
Feste
What ho, I say! Peace in this prison!
Sir Toby
The knave counterfeits well: a good knave.
Malvolio
20 [*Within*] Who calls there?
Feste
Sir Topas the curate, who comes to visit Malvolio the lunatic.
Malvolio
Sir Topas, Sir Topas, good Sir Topas, go to my lady!

24 *Out . . . fiend*: Feste addresses the imaginary devil possessing Malvolio. *hyperbolical*: overreaching, raging.

31 *modest*: moderate.
32 *use*: treat.
33 *house*: room.

35 *barricadoes*: barricades (which would shut out any light).
36 *clerestories*: upper windows. *south-north*: an intentionally meaningless direction.
38 *of obstruction*: that the light is shut out.

41 *puzzled*: bewildered.
41–2 *the Egyptians . . . fog*: A plague of 'black darkness' covered Egypt for three days (Exodus 10:21–3).

45 *abused*: badly treated.
46 *make the trial of it*: test my sanity. *constant question*: logical discussion.

47 *Pythagoras*: a Greek philosopher whose doctrine of the 'transmigration of souls' is correctly explained by Malvolio in the next line.
49 *grandam*: grandmother—i.e. ancestor. *haply*: perhaps.

Feste
Out, hyperbolical fiend! How vexest thou this man!
25 Talkest thou nothing but of ladies?

Sir Toby
Well said, Master Parson.

Malvolio
Sir Topas, never was man thus wronged. Good Sir Topas, do not think I am mad. They have laid me here in hideous darkness.

Feste
30 Fie, thou dishonest Satan! (I call thee by the most modest terms, for I am one of those gentle ones that will use the devil himself with courtesy.) Say'st thou that the house is dark?

Malvolio
As hell, Sir Topas.

Feste
35 Why, it hath bay-windows transparent as barricadoes, and the clerestories toward the south-north are as lustrous as ebony: and yet complainest thou of obstruction?

Malvolio
I am not mad, Sir Topas. I say to you, this house is dark.

Feste
40 Madman, thou errest. I say there is no darkness but ignorance, in which thou art more puzzled than the Egyptians in their fog.

Malvolio
I say this house is as dark as ignorance, though ignorance were as dark as hell; and I say there was never
45 man thus abused. I am no more mad than you are— make the trial of it in any constant question.

Feste
What is the opinion of Pythagoras concerning wildfowl?

Malvolio
That the soul of our grandam might haply inhabit a
50 bird.

Feste
What think'st thou of his opinion?

52 *I think nobly*: Malvolio holds the
Christian belief in the immortality of
the soul.

55 *hold*: believe.
55–6 *allow . . . wits*: certify your sanity.
56 *woodcock*: a proverbially foolish bird.
dispossess: dislodge.

60 *for all waters*: ready for anything.

61–2 *Thou . . . not*: The disguise had
been Maria's suggestion (*above*,
line 1).

63 *To him . . . voice*: now speak to him in
your own voice.
64–5 *I . . . knavery*: I wish we could get
this joke finished off.
65 *conveniently delivered*: released
without much trouble.
would: wish.
66 *so far in offence*: in so much trouble.
67 *upshot*: conclusion.
69 *Hey Robin*: an Elizabethan popular
song.

72 *perdie*: by God (French *par Dieu*).

Malvolio
I think nobly of the soul, and no way approve his
opinion.
Feste
Fare thee well: remain thou still in darkness. Thou shalt
55 hold th' opinion of Pythagoras ere I will allow of thy
wits, and fear to kill a woodcock lest thou dispossess the
soul of thy grandam. Fare thee well.
Malvolio
Sir Topas, Sir Topas!
Sir Toby
My most exquisite Sir Topas!
Feste
60 Nay, I am for all waters.
Maria
Thou might'st have done this without thy beard and
gown; he sees thee not.
Sir Toby
To him in thine own voice, and bring me word how
thou find'st him. I would we were well rid of this
65 knavery. If he may be conveniently delivered, I would he
were, for I am now so far in offence with my niece that I
cannot pursue with any safety this sport to the upshot.
Come by and by to my chamber.   [*Exit with* Maria
Feste
    Hey Robin, jolly Robin,
70   *Tell me how thy lady does.*
Malvolio
Fool!
Feste
    My lady is unkind, perdie.
Malvolio
Fool!
Feste
    Alas, why is she so?
Malvolio
75 Fool, I say!
Feste
    She loves another—Who calls, ha?

77 *as ever . . . hand*: if you ever want to do something for me which will be well rewarded.
78 *help me to*: fetch me.
79 *I will . . . for't*: as long as I live, I shall be grateful to you for this.

82 *besides*: out of.
five wits: mental faculties: common wit, imagination, fantasy, judgement, and memory.
83 *notoriously abused*: shamefully ill-treated.

85 *But as well*: only as well (i.e. no better than).

87 *propertied me*: treated me like a senseless object.
88–9 *to face . . . wits*: to drive me out of my mind.

90 *Advise you*: be careful.
91–2 *thy wits . . . restore*: may the heavens restore you to your right mind.
92 *endeavour . . . sleep*: try to get some sleep.
92–3 *vain bibble babble*: meaningless prattle.

95 *Maintain no words*: don't try to talk.
96 *God buy you*: God be with you.

100 *shent*: scolded.

Malvolio
Good fool, as ever thou wilt deserve well at my hand, help me to a candle, and pen, ink, and paper. As I am a gentleman, I will live to be thankful to thee for't.

Feste
80 Master Malvolio?

Malvolio
Ay, good fool.

Feste
Alas, sir, how fell you besides your five wits?

Malvolio
Fool, there was never man so notoriously abused! I am as well in my wits, fool, as thou art.

Feste
85 But as well? Then you are mad indeed, if you be no better in your wits than a fool.

Malvolio
They have here propertied me: keep me in darkness, send ministers to me—asses—and do all they can to face me out of my wits.

Feste
90 Advise you what you say: the minister is here. [*Speaking as* Sir Topas] Malvolio, Malvolio, thy wits the heavens restore: endeavour thyself to sleep, and leave thy vain bibble babble.

Malvolio
Sir Topas!

Feste
95 [*As* Sir Topas] Maintain no words with him, good fellow! [*As himself*] Who, I, sir? Not I, sir! God buy you, good Sir Topas! [*As* Sir Topas] Marry, amen! [*As himself*] I will, sir, I will.

Malvolio
Fool, fool, fool, I say!

Feste
100 Alas, sir, be patient. What say you, sir? I am shent for speaking to you.

Malvolio
Good fool, help me to some light and some paper: I tell thee I am as well in my wits as any man in Illyria.

104 *Well-a-day that*: alas, if only.

106 *convey . . . down*: carry the letter that I shall write.
106–7 *It shall . . . did*: you will get more for this than you have ever got for carrying letters.
109 *counterfeit*: pretend.

113 *requite it*: reward you for it.
in the highest degree: to the utmost.

115–22 *'I am gone . . . devil'*: Feste's song has not been identified.
115 *anon*: at once.
117 *trice*: moment.
the old Vice: a character in the Morality Plays of the fifteenth and sixteenth centuries, who belaboured the devil with his wooden sword and drove him from the stage.
118 *sustain*: satisfy.
121 *Pare*: cut.
123 *Adieu*: goodbye.
goodman: good master.

Act 4 Scene 3
Sebastian, already perplexed, is astonished when Olivia demands that he should marry her.

6 *there he was*: he had been there.
credit: information.
7 *range*: wander around.

Feste
Well-a-day that you were, sir!
Malvolio
105 By this hand, I am! Good fool, some ink, paper, and light, and convey what I will set down to my lady. It shall advantage thee more than ever the bearing of letter did.
Feste
I will help you to't. But tell me true, are you not mad indeed or do you but counterfeit?
Malvolio
110 Believe me, I am not. I tell thee true.
Feste
Nay, I'll ne'er believe a madman till I see his brains. I will fetch you light, and paper, and ink.
Malvolio
Fool, I'll requite it in the highest degree. I prithee, be gone.
Feste
115   *I am gone, sir, and anon, sir,*
       I'll be with you again,
    In a trice, like to the old Vice,
       Your need to sustain;
    Who, with dagger of lath, in his rage and his wrath,
120   *Cries, 'Ah, ha!' to the devil:*
    Like a mad lad, 'Pare thy nails, dad.
       Adieu, goodman devil!'   [*Exit*

Scene 3

Olivia's garden: enter Sebastian

Sebastian
This is the air, that is the glorious sun,
This pearl she gave me, I do feel't, and see't,
And though 'tis wonder that enwraps me thus,
Yet 'tis not madness. Where's Antonio then?
5 I could not find him at the Elephant.
Yet there he was, and there I found this credit,
That he did range the town to seek me out.

9 *my soul . . . sense*: my mind agrees with the evidence of my senses.
10 *this . . . madness*: there may be some mistake, but it's not madness.
11 *flood of fortune*: excess of good luck.
12 *instance*: precedent.
    discourse: explanation.
14 *wrangle*: argue.
15 *trust*: believe.

17 *sway*: govern, manage.
    followers: servants.
18 *Take . . . dispatch*: handle her household business and settle matters.
19 *With . . . bearing*: in such a calm, sensible, and poised manner.
21 *deceivable*: deceptive.

24 *chantry*: private chapel.
    by: near by.

26 *Plight . . . faith*: Olivia is demanding a 'troth-plight' before a witness, which would constitute a legally binding contract.
27 *jealous*: possessive.
    doubtful: insecure, suspicious.
28 *He*: the 'holy man'.
29 *Whiles*: until.
    come to note: be made public.
30-1 *What . . . birth*: when we will celebrate our wedding in a manner appropriate to my social position.
32-5 *I'll . . . mine*: The romantic, rhyming couplets signal the end of an episode.
35 *fairly note*: look favourably upon.

His counsel now might do me golden service:
For though my soul disputes well with my sense
10 That this may be some error, but no madness,
Yet doth this accident and flood of fortune
So far exceed all instance, all discourse,
That I am ready to distrust mine eyes,
And wrangle with my reason that persuades me
15 To any other trust but that I am mad,
Or else the lady's mad; yet if 'twere so,
She could not sway her house, command her followers,
Take and give back affairs and their dispatch,
With such a smooth, discreet, and stable bearing
20 As I perceive she does. There's something in't
That is deceivable. But here the lady comes.

Enter Olivia *and* Priest

Olivia
Blame not this haste of mine. If you mean well,
Now go with me and with this holy man
Into the chantry by; there before him,
25 And underneath that consecrated roof,
Plight me the full assurance of your faith,
That my most jealous and too doubtful soul
May live at peace. He shall conceal it
Whiles you are willing it shall come to note,
30 What time we will our celebration keep
According to my birth. What do you say?
Sebastian
I'll follow this good man, and go with you,
And having sworn truth, ever will be true.
Olivia
Then lead the way, good father, and heavens so shine,
35 That they may fairly note this act of mine!   [*Exeunt*

Act 5 Scene 1

Antonio is brought before Orsino, Olivia claims Viola/Cesario as her newly-betrothed husband, and Sir Toby and Sir Andrew complain about their encounter with Sebastian. The twins are reunited and two marriages are arranged. Malvolio is released from his prison.

1 *his*: i.e. Malvolio's letter to Olivia.

5–6 *give . . . again*: to give someone a gift, and ask to have it back again; see 'Source, Date, and Text', p.xix.

7 *Belong you to*: are you servants of.

8 *trappings*: ornaments.

15 *they*: my friends.
make an ass: make a fool of me.
16 *plainly*: honestly.

SCENE 1

The street: enter Feste *and* Fabian

Fabian
Now as thou lov'st me, let me see his letter.
Feste
Good Master Fabian, grant me another request.
Fabian
Anything.
Feste
Do not desire to see this letter.
Fabian
5 This is to give a dog, and in recompense desire my dog again.

Enter Orsino, Viola, Curio, *and* Lords

Orsino
Belong you to the Lady Olivia, friends?
Feste
Ay, sir, we are some of her trappings.
Orsino
I know thee well. How dost thou, my good fellow?
Feste
10 Truly, sir, the better for my foes, and the worse for my friends.
Orsino
Just the contrary: the better for thy friends.
Feste
No, sir: the worse.
Orsino
How can that be?
Feste
15 Marry, sir, they praise me, and make an ass of me. Now my foes tell me plainly I am an ass: so that by my foes,

17   *profit . . . myself*: gain self-knowledge.
18   *abused*: deceived, disgraced.
     conclusions . . . kisses: assuming that
     logical propositions are like kisses.
19   *your . . . affirmatives*: Grammatically
     speaking, two negatives make an
     affirmative ('no "no"' = 'yes').
     your: i.e. as you know.

23   *though*: even though.

26   *But . . . dealing*: except that it would
     be a) deceit; b) a second giving.
     I would: I wish.

29–30   *Put . . . obey it*: forget your honour
     ('grace') for the present, and give in to
     your human weakness.

33   *Primo . . . tertio*: first, second, third
     (Latin); requesting a third favour,
     Feste alludes to an elaborate
     mathematical contest, the
     'Philosopher's Game'.
     the old saying: i.e. 'third time lucky'—
     used to encourage gamblers to make
     another attempt.
34   *triplex*: triple time in music.
35   *tripping measure*: skipping rhythm.
     Saint Bennet: St Benedict's Church
     stood just opposite Shakespeare's
     Globe Theatre.
36   *put you in mind*: jog your memory.
37   *fool*: trick.
     throw: throw of the dice.
39   *bounty*: generosity.
41   *lullaby*: goodnight.
42–3   *my desire . . . covetousness*: Feste
     does not explain how these are
     different.
44   *anon*: very soon.

sir, I profit in the knowledge of myself, and by my
friends I am abused. So that, conclusions to be as kisses,
if your four negatives make your two affirmatives, why
20   then the worse for my friends, and the better for my
foes.

Orsino
Why, this is excellent.

Feste
By my troth, sir, no—though it please you to be one of
my friends.

Orsino
25   Thou shalt not be the worse for me: there's gold.

Feste
But that it would be double-dealing, sir, I would you
could make it another.

Orsino
O, you give me ill counsel.

Feste
Put your grace in your pocket, sir, for this once, and let
30   your flesh and blood obey it.

Orsino
Well, I will be so much a sinner to be a double-dealer;
there's another.

Feste
Primo, *secundo*, *tertio*, is a good play, and the old saying
is 'The third pays for all'; the triplex, sir, is a good
35   tripping measure; or the bells of Saint Bennet, sir, may
put you in mind—one, two, three.

Orsino
You can fool no more money out of me at this throw. If
you will let your lady know I am here to speak with her,
and bring her along with you, it may awake my bounty
40   further.

Feste
Marry, sir, lullaby to your bounty till I come again. I go,
sir, but I would not have you to think that my desire of
having is the sin of covetousness. But as you say, sir, let
your bounty take a nap, I will awake it anon.   [*Exit*

Enter Antonio *and* Officers

Viola

45 Here comes the man, sir, that did rescue me.

Orsino

That face of his I do remember well;
Yet when I saw it last, it was besmear'd
As black as Vulcan, in the smoke of war.
A baubling vessel was he captain of,

50 For shallow draught and bulk unprizable,
With which such scathful grapple did he make
With the most noble bottom of our fleet,
That very envy and the tongue of loss
Cried fame and honour on him. What's the matter?

First Officer

55 Orsino, this is that Antonio
That took the *Phoenix* and her fraught from Candy,
And this is he that did the *Tiger* board,
When your young nephew Titus lost his leg.
Here in the streets, desperate of shame and state,

60 In private brabble did we apprehend him.

Viola

He did me kindness, sir, drew on my side,
But in conclusion put strange speech upon me,
I know not what 'twas, but distraction.

48 *Vulcan*: the Roman god of
blacksmiths.
49 *baubling vessel*: miserable little boat.
50 *For . . . unprizable*: very lightweight
and not worth capturing.
draught: the depth of water needed to
float a vessel.
51 *such . . . make*: he engaged in such
destructive close fighting.
52 *bottom*: ship.
53 *very . . . loss*: even in our shame, and
with the voices of losers.
54 *Cried . . . him*: called out with praise
and honour for him.
56 *took*: captured.
fraught: freight, cargo.
Candy: Candia, capital of Crete.
59 *desperate . . . state*: regardless of
shame and danger.
60 *private brabble*: personal quarrel.
apprehend: arrest.
61 *drew . . . side*: drew his sword in my
defence.
62 *in conclusion*: afterwards.
put . . . upon me: spoke very oddly to
me.
63 *distraction*: madness.

64 *Notable*: notorious.
salt-water thief: robber on the seas.
65 *to their mercies*: into the hands of
those men.
66 *in terms . . . dear*: in such bloody and
deadly circumstances.

68 *Be . . . shake off*: please allow me to
deny.

70 *on base . . . enough*: with very good
reason.
71 *A witchcraft*: Sebastian has bewitched
Antonio—just as Olivia was enchanted
by Viola/Cesario (compare *3*, 1, 108).
72 *ingrateful*: ungrateful.
73 *rude*: rough.
74 *redeem*: rescue.
A wrack . . . was: he was hopelessly
shipwrecked.
76 *retention*: reservation.
77 *All . . . dedication*: I completely
devoted myself to him.
78 *pure*: only.
79 *adverse*: hostile.
80 *Drew*: drew my sword.
beset: attacked.
81 *being apprehended*: when I was
arrested.
82 *partake*: share.
83 *to face . . . acquaintance*: brazenly to
deny that he knew me.
84 *grew . . . thing*: became very distant.
removed: removèd.
85 *While . . . wink*: in the twinkling of an
eye.
denied: refused to give me.
86 *recommended*: committed.

89 *three months*: Shakespeare
manipulates the time scheme to suit
his own purposes.
90 *No int'rim*: without a break.
vacancy: space.
91 *keep company*: stay together.

92 *heaven . . . earth*: Orsino compares
Olivia to a goddess.

Orsino
Notable pirate, thou salt-water thief,
65 What foolish boldness brought thee to their mercies
Whom thou in terms so bloody and so dear
Hast made thine enemies?
Antonio
                                        Orsino, noble sir,
Be pleas'd that I shake off these names you give me:
Antonio never yet was thief, or pirate,
70 Though I confess, on base and ground enough,
Orsino's enemy. A witchcraft drew me hither:
That most ingrateful boy there by your side,
From the rude sea's enrag'd and foamy mouth
Did I redeem. A wrack past hope he was.
75 His life I gave him, and did thereto add
My love, without retention or restraint,
All his in dedication. For his sake
Did I expose myself—pure for his love—
Into the danger of this adverse town;
80 Drew to defend him, when he was beset;
Where being apprehended, his false cunning
(Not meaning to partake with me in danger)
Taught him to face me out of his acquaintance,
And grew a twenty years' removed thing
85 While one would wink; denied me mine own purse,
Which I had recommended to his use
Not half an hour before.
Viola
                                        How can this be?
Orsino
When came he to this town?
Antonio
Today, my lord and for three months before
90 No int'rim, not a minute's vacancy,
Both day and night did we keep company.

Enter Olivia *and* Attendants

Orsino
Here comes the Countess: now heaven walks on earth!
But for thee, fellow—fellow, thy words are madness.

94 *tended upon*: attended on.

95 *anon*: presently.

96 *but . . . have*: except that which he may not have (i.e. Olivia's love).
97 *seem serviceable*: be of assistance.
98 *keep promise*: i.e. to be true (*4*, 3, 33).

103 *aught . . . tune*: the same old stuff.
104 *fat and fulsome*: boring and sickening.
105 *howling*: the howling of a dog.

107 *uncivil*: rude, discourteous.

108 *ingrate*: ungrateful.
unauspicious: unrewarding.

110 *e'er devotion tender'd*: ever offered in devotion.

111 *Even what*: whatever.
become: be suitable.

113 *th' Egyptian thief*: An Egyptian bandit threatened by death (in a story by Heliodorus) tried to kill a captive whom he loved.

115 *savours nobly*: has a noble air.
hear me this: just let me say this.
116 *to non-regardance*: into disregard.
117 *that*: since.
partly know: have some idea of.
118 *screws*: wrests.
119 *marble-breasted*: hard-hearted.
120 *minion*: darling, favourite.
121 *tender*: hold, care for.

Three months this youth hath tended upon me;
95 But more of that anon. Take him aside.
    Olivia
What would my lord—but that he may not have—
Wherein Olivia may seem serviceable?
Cesario, you do not keep promise with me.
    Viola
Madam?
    Orsino
100 Gracious Olivia—
    Olivia
What do you say, Cesario? [*To* Orsino] Good my
    lord—
    Viola
My lord would speak; my duty hushes me.
    Olivia
If it be aught to the old tune, my lord,
It is as fat and fulsome to mine ear
105 As howling after music.
    Orsino
Still so cruel?
    Olivia
                Still so constant, lord.
    Orsino
What, to perverseness? You uncivil lady,
To whose ingrate and unauspicious altars
My soul the faithfull'st off'rings hath breath'd out
110 That e'er devotion tender'd—What shall I do?
    Olivia
Even what it please my lord that shall become him.
    Orsino
Why should I not, had I the heart to do it,
Like to th' Egyptian thief at point of death,
Kill what I love?—a savage jealousy
115 That sometimes savours nobly! But hear me this:
Since you to non-regardance cast my faith,
And that I partly know the instrument
That screws me from my true place in your favour,
Live you the marble-breasted tyrant still.
120 But this your minion, whom I know you love,
And whom, by heaven, I swear I tender dearly,

122 *cruel*: i.e. towards Orsino.
123 *he . . . spite*: he gets the high honour that his master should have.
       crowned: crownèd.
124 *ripe in mischief*: ready to do injury.
126 *a raven . . . dove*: a black heart in a fair body.
127 *jocund*: cheerful.
       apt: ready.
128 *do you rest*: give you peace.

131 *by all mores*: by all comparatives.
       love wife: love a wife.
132 *feign*: pretend.
       witnesses above: gods.
133 *tainting*: discrediting.
134 *Ay me detested*: Oh I am accursed.
       beguil'd: deceived.
135 *do you wrong*: injure you.

140 *sirrah*: a contemptuous form of address.
141 *the baseness . . . fear*: your miserable cowardice.
142 *strangle thy propriety*: suppress your real identity (i.e. as Olivia's husband).
143 *take . . . up*: assume your proper place in life.
144 *Be that*: be what.
145 *as that thou fear'st*: as great as the man (i.e. Orsino) that you are afraid of.

Him will I tear out of that cruel eye
Where he sits crowned in his master's spite.
Come, boy, with me; my thoughts are ripe in mischief:
125 I'll sacrifice the lamb that I do love,
To spite a raven's heart within a dove.
       Viola
And I most jocund, apt, and willingly,
To do you rest, a thousand deaths would die.
       Olivia
Where goes Cesario?
       Viola
                                   After him I love
130 More than I love these eyes, more than my life,
More, by all mores, than e'er I shall love wife.
If I do feign, you witnesses above
Punish my life, for tainting of my love.
       Olivia
Ay me detested! How am I beguil'd!
       Viola
135 Who does beguile you? Who does do you wrong?
       Olivia
Hast thou forgot thyself? Is it so long?
Call forth the holy father.   [*Exit an* Attendant
       Orsino
                                   Come, away!
       Olivia
Whither, my lord? Cesario, husband, stay!
       Orsino
Husband?
       Olivia
                     Ay, husband. Can he that deny?
       Orsino
140 Her husband, sirrah?
       Viola
                              No, my lord, not I.
       Olivia
Alas, it is the baseness of thy fear
That makes thee strangle thy propriety.
Fear not, Cesario, take thy fortunes up,
Be that thou know'st thou art, and then thou art
145 As great as that thou fear'st.

Enter Priest

O welcome, father!
Father, I charge thee by thy reverence
Here to unfold—though lately we intended
To keep in darkness what occasion now
Reveals before 'tis ripe—what thou dost know
150 Hath newly pass'd between this youth and me.

Priest
A contract of eternal bond of love,
Confirm'd by mutual joinder of your hands,
Attested by the holy close of lips,
Strengthen'd by interchangement of your rings,
155 And all the ceremony of this compact
Seal'd in my function, by my testimony;
Since when, my watch hath told me, toward my grave
I have travell'd but two hours.

Orsino
O thou dissembling cub! What wilt thou be
160 When time hath sow'd a grizzle on thy case?
Or will not else thy craft so quickly grow
That thine own trip shall be thine overthrow?
Farewell, and take her; but direct thy feet
Where thou and I henceforth may never meet.

Viola
165 My lord, I do protest—

Olivia
O do not swear!
Hold little faith, though thou hast too much fear.

Enter Sir Andrew

Sir Andrew
For the love of God, a surgeon! Send one presently to Sir
Toby.

Olivia
What's the matter?

Sir Andrew
170 'Has broke my head across, and has given Sir Toby a
bloody coxcomb too. For the love of God, your help! I
had rather than forty pound I were at home.

---

146 *charge*: order.
by thy reverence: in all your holiness.
147 *unfold*: reveal.
lately: recently.
148 *in darkness*: hidden.
occasion: the circumstances.
150 *newly pass'd*: recently taken place.

152 *joinder*: joining.
153 *Attested*: demonstrated.
the holy close of lips: a holy kiss.
154 *interchangement*: exchange.

156 *Seal'd in my function*: made official by me as a priest.
testimony: formal statement.
157–8 *toward . . . hours*: I am only two hours older.
159 *dissembling cub*: lying little fox.
160 *sow'd . . . case*: scattered grey hairs on your head ('case' = fox-skin).
161 *craft*: cunning skill.
162 *trip*: a wrestling term for the movement that throws an opponent to the ground.
163–4 *direct . . . meet*: make sure we never meet again.

166 *Hold little faith*: keep some part of your promise.

167 *presently*: immediately.

170 *'Has . . . across*: he has hit me over the head; apparently there has been a second bout of skirmishing not shown onstage.
171 *coxcomb*: head.
171–2 *I had . . . home*: I would give a lot of money to be at home; 'forty' = an unspecified large sum.

174 *took him for*: thought he was.
175 *incardinate*: in the flesh; Sir Andrew
    means 'incarnate'.

177 *'Od's lifelings*: by God's little lives (a
    mild oath).
177–8 *for nothing*: for no reason.
178–9 *that . . . Sir Toby*: it was Sir Toby
    who made me do what I did.

182 *bespake you fair*: answered you
    courteously.

184 *set nothing by*: think nothing of.
185 *halting*: limping.
186 *in drink*: drunk.
186–7 *tickled . . . did*: dealt with you
    differently.

Olivia
Who has done this, Sir Andrew?
Sir Andrew
The Count's gentleman, one Cesario. We took him for a
175 coward, but he's the very devil incardinate.
Orsino
My gentleman, Cesario?
Sir Andrew
'Od's lifelings, here he is! You broke my head for
nothing; and that that I did, I was set on to do't by Sir
Toby.
Viola
180 Why do you speak to me? I never hurt you.
You drew your sword upon me without cause,
But I bespake you fair, and hurt you not.

Enter Sir Toby *and* Feste

Sir Andrew
If a bloody coxcomb be a hurt, you have hurt me: I
think you set nothing by a bloody coxcomb. Here comes
185 Sir Toby halting; you shall hear more. But if he had not
been in drink, he would have tickled you othergates
than he did.

188 *How is't with you*: what's wrong with
you.

189 *That's . . . on't*: it doesn't matter: he's
hurt me, and that's that.
190 *Sot*: you drunken fool.
Dick Surgeon: Dick the surgeon.
191 *an hour agone*: for the past hour.
191–2 *set . . . morning*: glazed over (in
drunkenness) at eight o'clock this
morning.
193 *passy-measures pavin*: The 'passe-
measure pavane' was a stately dance.

196 *be dressed*: have our wounds dressed.

198 *gull*: dupe.
199 *looked to*: taken care of.
201 *brother . . . blood*: my own brother.
202 *with . . . safety*: with any sensible
concern for my own safety.
203 *throw . . . me*: look upon me strangely.
205 *even for*: especially because of.
206 *but . . . ago*: so recently.
207 *One*: the same.
habit: costume; Viola explained
(*3*, *4*, *356*) that she imitated
Sebastian in 'fashion, colour,
ornament').
208 *A natural perspective*: an optical
illusion produced by nature (not by
mirrors).

210 *rack'd*: dragged out (as though he
were tortured on the rack).

Orsino
How now, gentleman? How is't with you?
  Sir Toby
That's all one; 'has hurt me, and there's th' end on't.
190 Sot, didst see Dick Surgeon, sot?
  Feste
O, he's drunk, Sir Toby, an hour agone; his eyes were set
at eight i' th' morning.
  Sir Toby
Then he's a rogue, and a passy-measures pavin. I hate a
drunken rogue.
  Olivia
195 Away with him! Who hath made this havoc with them?
  Sir Andrew
I'll help you, Sir Toby, because we'll be dressed together.
  Sir Toby
Will you help? An ass-head, and a coxcomb, and a
knave, a thin-faced knave, a gull!
  Olivia
Get him to bed, and let his hurt be looked to.
    [*Exeunt* Feste, Fabian, Sir Toby, *and* Sir Andrew

Enter Sebastian

  Sebastian
200 I am sorry, madam, I have hurt your kinsman:
But had it been the brother of my blood,
I must have done no less with wit and safety.
You throw a strange regard upon me, and by that
I do perceive it hath offended you:
205 Pardon me, sweet one, even for the vows
We made each other but so late ago.
  Orsino
One face, one voice, one habit, and two persons!
A natural perspective, that is, and is not!
  Sebastian
Antonio! O my dear Antonio,
210 How have the hours rack'd and tortur'd me,
Since I have lost thee!
  Antonio
Sebastian are you?

212 *Fear'st thou*: do you doubt.

213 *made . . . yourself*: divided yourself in two.
214 *cleft*: split.

218–19 *Nor . . . everywhere*: and I don't have the divine power of being omnipresent.
220 *blind*: unseeing, pitiless.
221 *Of charity*: be kind and tell me.
kin: relation.
222 *What countryman*: what is your nationality.

225 *suited*: dressed.
226 *If spirits . . . suit*: if ghosts can appear in human form and clothing.

227 *spirit . . . indeed*: I certainly have an immortal soul.
228–9 *am . . . participate*: have the same physical earthly form that I was born with.
230 *as . . . even*: as it appears from everything else (except the dress).
232 *drowned*: drownèd.

235–6 *died . . . years*: died on my thirteenth birthday.

237 *record*: recollection.
lively: vivid.
238 *finished*: finishèd.
his mortal act: his life.

Sebastian
                    Fear'st thou that, Antonio?
Antonio
How have you made division of yourself?
An apple cleft in two is not more twin
215 Than these two creatures. Which is Sebastian?
Olivia
Most wonderful!
Sebastian
Do I stand there? I never had a brother;
Nor can there be that deity in my nature
Of here and everywhere. I had a sister,
220 Whom the blind waves and surges have devour'd.
Of charity, what kin are you to me?
What countryman? What name? What parentage?
Viola
Of Messaline. Sebastian was my father;
Such a Sebastian was my brother too:
225 So went he suited to his watery tomb.
If spirits can assume both form and suit,
You come to fright us.
Sebastian
                    A spirit I am indeed,
But am in that dimension grossly clad
Which from the womb I did participate.
230 Were you a woman, as the rest goes even,
I should my tears let fall upon your cheek
And say, 'Thrice welcome, drowned Viola.'
Viola
My father had a mole upon his brow.
Sebastian
And so had mine.
Viola
235 And died that day when Viola from her birth
Had number'd thirteen years.
Sebastian
O, that record is lively in my soul!
He finished indeed his mortal act
That day that made my sister thirteen years.

240 *lets*: hinders.
241 *this . . . attire*: the male clothing I have no right to wear.

243 *cohere and jump*: concur and agree.

246 *maiden weeds*: female garments. *whose*: i.e. the captain's.

248 *All . . . since*: everything that has happened to me since then.
249 *between*: concerned with.

250 *So . . . mistook*: that's why you made this mistake, my lady.
251 *nature . . . that*: nature corrected that mistake in her own way; the 'bias', in the game of bowls, is the lead weighting that influences the bowl's progress.
253 *by my life*: upon my life.
254 *a maid and man*: a virgin youth.
255 *amaz'd*: bewildered.
    right . . . blood: he is of truly noble birth.
256 *true*: accurate, not a distorting mirror.
257 *most happy wreck*: very fortunate shipwreck.
259 *like to me*: as you love me.
260 *over-swear*: swear over again.

262 *As doth . . . fire*: as truly as the sphere of the sun maintains its fire.
263 *severs*: divides.

266 *action*: legal charge.
267 *in durance*: imprisoned.
    at Malvolio's suit: on the accusation of Malvolio.
268 *follower*: servant.
269 *enlarge him*: set him free.
270 *I remember me*: I remember.
271 *distract*: disturbed in his mind.

Viola
240 If nothing lets to make us happy both,
But this my masculine usurp'd attire,
Do not embrace me, till each circumstance
Of place, time, fortune, do cohere and jump
That I am Viola; which to confirm
245 I'll bring you to a captain in this town,
Where lie my maiden weeds; by whose gentle help
I was preserv'd to serve this noble Count.
All the occurrence of my fortune since
Hath been between this lady and this lord.
Sebastian
250 [*To* Olivia] So comes it, lady, you have been mistook.
But nature to her bias drew in that.
You would have been contracted to a maid;
Nor are you therein, by my life, deceiv'd:
You are betroth'd both to a maid and man.
Orsino
255 Be not amaz'd; right noble is his blood.
If this be so, as yet the glass seems true,
I shall have share in this most happy wreck.
[*To* Viola] Boy, thou hast said to me a thousand times
Thou never should'st love woman like to me.
Viola
260 And all those sayings will I over-swear,
And all those swearings keep as true in soul
As doth that orbed continent the fire
That severs day from night.
Orsino   Give me thy hand,
And let me see thee in thy woman's weeds.
Viola
265 The captain that did bring me first on shore
Hath my maid's garments. He upon some action
Is now in durance at Malvolio's suit,
A gentleman and follower of my lady's.
Olivia
He shall enlarge him: fetch Malvolio hither.
270 And yet alas, now I remember me,
They say, poor gentleman, he's much distract.

272 *A . . . own*: my own distracting madness.
275 *he holds . . . end*: he is keeping the devil ('Beelzebub') at the end of his staff (= at a safe distance); the metaphor is from fighting with staves.
276 *case*: condition.
   'Has: he has.
277 *today morning*: this morning.
278 *epistles*: a) love-letters; b) Epistles of the New Testament of the Bible.
   gospels: a) the first four books of the New Testament; b) unquestionable truths.
   it . . . delivered: it doesn't matter in which order they are read; specific times were set in church services for the reading of the Gospels.
279 *delivered*: a) handed over; b) narrated.
281 *Look . . . edified*: prepare to be (spiritually) instructed.
   delivers: speaks for.
284 *do but read*: only read.
   an': if.

285 *vox*: voice (Latin), the proper pitch and intonation.
286 *i' thy right wits*: in your usual way.
287–8 *to read . . . thus*: to read Malvolio's 'right wits' is to read like this.
287 *his*: Malvolio's.
288 *perpend*: pay attention.
292 *rule*: authority.
294 *induced*: persuaded.
295 *semblance*: appearance.
297–8 *I leave . . . unthought of*: I rather forget my manners.
298 *out . . . injury*: from my sense of injury.

Enter Feste *with a letter, and* Fabian

A most extracting frenzy of mine own
From my remembrance clearly banish'd his.
How does he, sirrah?

Feste

275 Truly, Madam, he holds Beelzebub at the stave's end as
well as a man in his case may do. 'Has here writ a letter
to you—I should have given't you today morning, but
as a madman's epistles are no gospels, so it skills not
much when they are delivered.

Olivia

280 Open't, and read it.

Feste

Look then to be well edified, when the fool delivers the
madman. [*Reads like a madman*] By the Lord, madam—

Olivia

How now, art thou mad?

Feste

No, madam, I do but read madness: an' your ladyship
285 will have it as it ought to be, you must allow *vox*.

Olivia

Prithee, read i' thy right wits.

Feste

So I do, madonna. But to read his right wits is to read
thus: therefore, perpend, my princess, and give ear.

Olivia

[*To* Fabian] Read it you, sirrah.

Fabian

[*Reads*]

290   *By the Lord, madam, you wrong me, and the world*
   shall know it. Though you have put me into
   darkness, and given your drunken cousin rule over
   me, yet have I the benefit of my senses as well as
   your ladyship. I have your own letter that induced
295   *me to the semblance I put on; with the which I*
   doubt not but to do myself much right, or you much
   shame. Think of me as you please. I leave my duty a
   little unthought of, and speak out of my injury.
                        The madly-used Malvolio

Olivia

300   Did he write this?

Feste

Ay, madam.

Orsino

This savours not much of distraction.

Olivia

See him deliver'd, Fabian, bring him hither.

> [*Exit* Fabian

My lord, so please you, these things further thought
    on,

305   To think me as well a sister, as a wife;

One day shall crown th' alliance on't, so please you,

Here at my house, and at my proper cost.

Orsino

Madam, I am most apt t'embrace your offer.

[*To* Viola] Your master quits you; and for your service
    done him,

310   So much against the mettle of your sex,

So far beneath your soft and tender breeding,

And since you call'd me master for so long,

Here is my hand; you shall from this time be

Your master's mistress.

Olivia

A sister! You are she.

Enter Fabian *with* Malvolio

Orsino

315   Is this the madman?

Olivia

Ay, my lord, this same.

How now, Malvolio?

Malvolio

Madam, you have done me wrong,

Notorious wrong.

Olivia

Have I, Malvolio? No!

Malvolio

Lady, you have. Pray you, peruse that letter.

You must not now deny it is your hand:

---

302 *savours . . . distraction*: doesn't sound much like madness.

303 *deliver'd*: released.

304–5 *so please . . . wife*: won't you please, now that we have thought about these matters, look on me as a sister, not a wife.

306 *One day . . . on't*: the same (wedding) day shall celebrate the relationship.

307 *proper*: own.

308 *apt*: ready.

310 *mettle*: nature.

311 *soft . . . breeding*: gentle upbringing.

314 *A sister*: Olivia will now have a sister—as well as a brother.

317 *notorious*: outrageous.

318 *peruse*: study.

319 *hand*: handwriting.

320 *from it*: differently.
   in . . . phrase: in handwriting or style.
321 *invention*: composition.
322 *grant*: admit.
323 *in the modesty of honour*: decently and honourably.
324 *clear lights*: unmistakable signs.
325 *Bade*: ordered.

327 *lighter*: inferior.
328 *acting this*: when I did this.
329 *suffer'd*: allowed.
330 *the priest*: i.e. 'Sir Topas'.
331 *geck and gull*: fool and dupe.
332 *invention*: trickery.

334 *character*: handwriting.
335 *out of question*: without a doubt.
   hand: handwriting.
336 *bethink me*: remember.
337 *then cam'st*: then you came.
338 *forms*: ways.
   presuppos'd: earlier enjoined.
340 *This . . . thee*: this trick has been played on you most mischievously.
341 *grounds*: reasons.
   authors: those responsible.

344 *to come*: in future.
345 *Taint*: spoil.
   condition: happiness.
346 *wonder'd*: marvelled.
348 *Set . . . against*: played this trick on Malvolio.
349–50 *Upon . . . him*: because of some harsh and discourteous behaviour we had attributed to him.
350 *writ*: wrote.
351 *importance*: importunity.
352 *In recompense whereof*: as a reward for which.
353 *How . . . follow'd*: how it was carried out like a naughty game.
354 *pluck on*: provoke.
355 *If that*: if.
   justly: fairly.
356 *pass'd*: been suffered.

320 Write from it, if you can, in hand or phrase,
Or say 'tis not your seal, not your invention.
You can say none of this. Well, grant it then,
And tell me, in the modesty of honour,
Why you have given me such clear lights of favour,
325 Bade me come smiling and cross-garter'd to you,
To put on yellow stockings, and to frown
Upon Sir Toby, and the lighter people?
And acting this in an obedient hope,
Why have you suffer'd me to be imprison'd,
330 Kept in a dark house, visited by the priest,
And made the most notorious geck and gull
That e'er invention play'd on? Tell me, why?
   Olivia
Alas, Malvolio, this is not my writing,
Though I confess much like the character:
335 But, out of question, 'tis Maria's hand.
And now I do bethink me, it was she
First told me thou wast mad; then cam'st in smiling,
And in such forms which here were presuppos'd
Upon thee in the letter. Prithee, be content;
340 This practice hath most shrewdly pass'd upon thee.
But when we know the grounds and authors of it,
Thou shalt be both the plaintiff and the judge
Of thine own cause.
   Fabian
                     Good madam, hear me speak,
And let no quarrel, nor no brawl to come,
345 Taint the condition of this present hour,
Which I have wonder'd at. In hope it shall not,
Most freely I confess, myself and Toby
Set this device against Malvolio here,
Upon some stubborn and uncourteous parts
350 We had conceiv'd against him. Maria writ
The letter, at Sir Toby's great importance,
In recompense whereof he hath married her.
How with a sportful malice it was follow'd
May rather pluck on laughter than revenge,
355 If that the injuries be justly weigh'd
That have on both sides pass'd.

357 *baffled*: humiliated.

360 *interlude*: entertainment.
one Sir Topas: a certain Sir Topas.
that's all one: that isn't important.
362–3 *'Madam . . . gagged'*: Feste recalls
Malvolio's words early in the play
(*1, 5, 75–9*).
363 *whirligig*: spinning-top.
364 *his*: its.

366 *notoriously abus'd*: shamefully
misused.

368 *the captain*: the captain who keeps
Viola's 'maiden weeds' (line 246).
369 *convents*: is convenient.
370 *solemn combination*: formal union.
371 *sweet sister*: Orsino accepts Olivia's
invitation (lines 306–7).

374 *habits*: clothes (i.e. her female dress).
375 *fancy's*: love's.

376 *When . . . and*: when I was only.

378 *A foolish . . . toy*: a silly trick was
accepted as something trivial.

380 *came to man's estate*: grew up to be a
man.

384 *to wive*: to take a wife.

Olivia
Alas, poor fool, how have they baffled thee!
　　Feste
Why, 'Some are born great, some achieve greatness, and
some have greatness thrown upon them.' I was one, sir,
360 in this interlude, one Sir Topas, sir—but that's all one.
'By the Lord, fool, I am not mad.' But do you remember:
'Madam, why laugh you at such a barren rascal; an' you
smile not, he's gagged'? And thus the whirligig of time
brings in his revenges.
　　Malvolio
365 I'll be reveng'd on the whole pack of you! 　　　[*Exit*
　　Olivia
He hath been most notoriously abus'd.
　　Orsino
Pursue him, and entreat him to a peace.
He hath not told us of the captain yet. 　　[*Exit* Fabian
When that is known, and golden time convents,
370 A solemn combination shall be made
Of our dear souls. Meantime, sweet sister,
We will not part from hence. Cesario, come—
For so you shall be while you are a man.
But when in other habits you are seen.
375 Orsino's mistress, and his fancy's queen.
　　　　　　　　　[*Exeunt all except* Feste
　　Feste
When that I was and a little tiny boy,
　　With hey, ho, the wind and the rain,
A foolish thing was but a toy,
　　For the rain it raineth every day.

380 *But when I came to man's estate,*
　　With hey, ho, the wind and the rain,
'Gainst knaves and thieves men shut their gate,
　　For the rain it raineth every day.

But when I came, alas, to wive,
385　*With hey, ho, the wind and the rain,*
By swaggering could I never thrive,
　　For the rain it raineth every day.

388 *came . . . beds*: got much older.

390 *With . . . heads*: like other drunkards I
always had a hangover.

394 *that's all one*: that doesn't matter now.

395 *we'll strive . . . day*: the signal for the
audience to applaud.

But when I came unto my beds,
 With hey, ho, the wind and the rain,
With toss-pots still 'had drunken heads,   390
 For the rain it raineth every day.

A great while ago the world begun,
 With hey, ho, the wind and the rain,
But that's all one, our play is done,
 And we'll strive to please you every day.   395

[Exit

The Songs in Twelfth Night

O mistress mine

1. O mis - tress mine, where are you roam-ing?
2. What __ is love? 'Tis not here - af - ter,

O stay and hear, your true love's co - ming, O stay and
Pre - sent mirth hath pre - sent laugh-ter: Pre - sent

hear, your true love's co - ming, That can sing both high and
mirth hath pre - sent laugh - ter: What's to come is still un -

low. Trip __ no fur - ther, pret - ty sweet-ing: Jour - neys
- sure. In __ de - lay there lies no plen - ty, Then __ come

end in lo - vers meet - ing, Ev-'ry wise man's son doth know.
kiss me, sweet and twen - ty: Youth's a stuff will not en - dure.

When that I was

When that I was and a lit - tle ti - ny boy, With a

hey - ho, the wind __ and the rain, A fool - ish thing was

but __ a __ toy, For the rain it rain - eth

ev - 'ry __ day, With a hey - ho, the

wind and the rain, For the rain it rain - eth ev - 'ry __ day.

Background

England in 1600

When Shakespeare was writing *Twelfth Night*, many people still believed that the sun went round the earth. They were taught that this was the way God had ordered things, and that – in England – God had founded a Church and appointed a Monarchy so that the land and people could be well governed.

'The past is a foreign country; they do things differently there.'

L. P. Hartley

Government For most of Shakespeare's life, the reigning monarch of England was Queen Elizabeth I. With her counsellors and ministers, she governed the nation from London, although fewer than half a million people out of a total population of six million lived in the capital city. In the rest of the country, law and order were maintained by the land-owners and enforced by their deputies. The average man had no vote, and women had no rights at all.

Religion At this time, England was a Christian country. All children were baptized, soon after they were born, into the Church of England; they were taught the essentials of the Christian faith, and instructed in their duty to God and to humankind. Marriages and funerals were conducted only by the licensed clergy and according to the Church's rites and ceremonies. Attending divine service was compulsory; absences (without a good medical reason) could be punished by fines. By such means, the authorities were able to keep some control over the population – recording births, marriages, and deaths; being alert to anyone who refused to accept standard religious practices, who could be politically dangerous; and ensuring that people received the approved teachings through the official 'Homilies' which were regularly preached in all parish churches.

Elizabeth I's father, Henry VIII, had broken away from the Church of Rome, and from that time all people in England were able to hear the church services *in their own language* rather than in Latin. The Book of Common Prayer was used in every church, and an English traslation of the Bible was read aloud in public. The Christian religion had never been so well taught before!

Education

School education reinforced the Church's teaching. From the age of four, boys might attend the 'petty school' (its name came from the French '*petite école*' to learn reading and writing along with a few prayers; some schools also included work with numbers. At the age of seven, boys were ready for the grammar schools (if their fathers were willing and able to pay the fees).

Grammar schools taught Latin grammar, translation work and the study of Roman authors, paying attention as much to style as to content. The art of fine writing was therefore important from early youth. A very few students went on to university; these were either clever boys who won scholarships, or else the sons of rich noblemen. Girls stayed at home, and learned domestic and social skills – cooking, sewing, perhaps even music. The lucky ones might learn to read and write.

Language

At the start of the sixteenth century the English had a very poor opinion of their own language: there was little serious writing in English, and hardly any literature. Latin was the language of international scholarship, and the eloquent style of the Romans was much admired. Many translations from Latin were made, and in this way writers increased the vocabulary of English and made its grammar more flexible. French, Italian, and Spanish works were also translated and, for the first time, there were English versions of the Bible. By the end of the century, English was a language to be proud of: it was rich in vocabulary, capable of infinite variety and subtlety, and ready for all kinds of word-play – especially *puns*, for which Elizabethan English is renowned.

Drama

The great art-form of the Elizabethan and Jacobean age was its drama. The Elizabethans inherited a tradition of play-acting from the Middle Ages, and they reinforced this by reading and translating the Roman playwrights. At the beginning of the sixteenth century plays were performed by groups of actors. These were all-male companies (boys acted the female roles) who travelled from town to town, setting up their stages in open places (such as inn-yards) or, with the permission of the owner, in the hall of some noble house. The touring companies continued outside London into the seventeenth century; but in London, in 1576, a new building was erected for the performance of plays. This was the Theatre, the first purpose-built playhouse in England. Other playhouses followed, including the Globe, where most of Shakespeare's plays were performed, and English drama reached new heights.

There were people who disapproved, of course. The theatres, which brought large crowds together, could encourage the spread of disease – and dangerous ideas. During the summer, when the plague was at its worst, the playhouses were closed. A constant censorship was imposed, more or less severe at different times. The Puritans, a religious and political faction who wanted to impose strict rules of behaviour, tried to close down the theatres. However, partly because the royal family favoured drama, and partly because the buildings were outside the city limits, they did not succeed until 1642.

Theatre From contemporary comments and sketches – most particularly a drawing by a Dutch visitor, Johannes de Witt – it is possible to form some idea of the typical Elizabethan playhouse for which most of Shakespeare's plays were written. Hexagonal (six-sided) in shape, it had three roofed galleries encircling an open courtyard. The plain, high stage projected into the yard, where it was surrounded by the audience of standing 'groundings'. At the back were two doors for the actors' entrances and exits; and above these doors was a balcony – useful for a musicians' gallery or for the acting of scenes '*above*'. Over the stage was a thatched roof, supported on two pillars, forming a canopy – which seems to have been painted with the sun, moon, and stars for the 'heavens'.

Underneath was space (concealed by curtains) which could be used by characters ascending and descending through a trapdoor in the stage. Costumes and properties were kept backstage in the 'tiring house'. The actors used the most luxurious costumes they could find, often clothes given to them by rich patrons. Stage properties were important for showing where a scene was set, but the dramatist's own words were needed to explain the time of day, since all performances took place in the early afternoon.

A replica of Shakespeare's own theatre, the Globe, has been built in London, and stands in Southwark, almost exactly on the Bankside site of the original.

William Shakespeare, 1564–1616

Elizabeth I was Queen of England when Shakespeare was born in 1564. He was the son of a tradesman who made and sold gloves in the small town of Stratford-upon-Avon, and he was educated at the grammar school in that town. Shakespeare did not go to university when he left school, but worked, perhaps, in his father's business. When he was eighteen he married Anne Hathaway, who became the mother of his daughter, Susanna, in 1583, and of twins in 1585.

There is nothing exciting, or even unusual, in this story; and from 1585 until 1592 there are no documents that can tell us anything at all about Shakespeare. But we have learned that in 1592 he was known in London, and that he had become both an actor and a playwright.

We do not know when Shakespeare wrote his first play, and indeed we are not sure of the order in which he wrote his works. If you look on page 108 at the list of his writings and their approximate dates, you will see how he started by writing plays on subjects taken from the history of England. No doubt this was partly because he was always an intensely patriotic man – but he was also a very shrewd businessman. He could see that the theatre audiences enjoyed being shown their own history, and it was certain that he would make a profit from this kind of drama.

The plays in the next group are mainly comedies, with romantic love-stories of young people who fall in love with one another, and at the end of the play marry and live happily ever after. *Twelfth Night* is the last of these.

At the end of the sixteenth century the happiness disappears, and Shakespeare's plays become melancholy, bitter, and tragic. This change may have been caused by some sadness in the writer's life (one of his twins died in 1596). Shakespeare, however, was not the only writer whose works at this time were very serious. The whole of England was facing a crisis. Queen Elizabeth I was growing old. She was greatly loved, and the people were sad to think she must soon die; they were also afraid, for the queen had never married, and so there was no child to succeed her.

When James I came to the throne in 1603, Shakespeare continued to write serious drama – the great tragedies and the plays based on Roman history (such as *Julius Caesar*) for which he is most famous. Finally, before he retired from the theatre, he wrote another set of comedies.

These all have the same theme: they tell of happiness which is lost, and then found again.

Shakespeare returned from London to Stratford, his home town. He was rich and successful, and he owned one of the biggest houses in the town. He died in 1616. Although several of his plays were published separately, most of them (including *Twelfth Night*) were not printed until 1623, in a collection known as 'the First Folio'.

Shakespeare also wrote two long poems, and a collection of sonnets. The sonnets describe two love-affairs, but we do not know who the lovers were. Although there are many public documents concerned with his career as a writer and a businessman, Shakespeare has hidden his personal life from us. A nineteenth-century poet, Matthew Arnold, addressed Shakespeare in a poem, and wrote 'We ask and ask – Thou smilest, and art still'.

There is not even a trustworthy portrait of the world's greatest dramatist.

Approximate Dates of Composition of Shakespeare's Works

Period	Comedies	History plays	Tragedies	Poems
I 1594	Comedy of Errors Taming of the Shrew Two Gentlemen of Verona Love's Labour's Lost	Henry VI, part 1 Henry VI, part 2 Henry VI, part 3 Richard III King John	Titus Andronicus	Venus and Adonis Rape of Lucrece
II 1599	Midsummer Night's Dream Merchant of Venice Merry Wives of Windsor Much Ado About Nothing As You Like It	Richard II Henry IV, part 1 Henry IV, part 2 Henry V	Romeo and Juliet	Sonnets
III 1608	Twelfth Night Troilus and Cressida Measure for Measure All's Well That Ends Well		Julius Caesar Hamlet Othello Timon of Athens King Lear Macbeth Antony and Cleopatra Coriolanus	
IV 1613	Pericles Cymbeline The Winter's Tale The Tempest	Henry VIII		

Exploring Twelfth Night in the Classroom

Twelfth Night is a play about love, disguises, misunderstandings, mischief and fun. Like the best comedies, it works on different levels and it has something for all ages, so students will find plenty to enjoy in this play.

This section will suggest a range of approaches in the classroom, to help bring the text to life and to engender both enjoyment and understanding of the play.

Ways into the Play

Students may feel an antipathy towards the study of Shakespeare. The imaginative and enthusiastic teacher, with the help of this edition of the play, will soon break this down!

Twelfth Night

The Christian feast of Epiphany, Twelfth Night, is the day we associate with the Christmas tree coming down and decorations being put away. It's the last day of the Christmas season of festivities and therefore a last opportunity to make merry and have fun. Ask students to consider the types of ingredients that would be suitable for a play being performed at this time of year.

Every picture tells a story

Ask your students to look at some pictures related to *Twelfth Night* – for example, the picture on the front cover of this book, or paintings from the Shakespeare Illustrated site (see p. 118) – and guess who the people are and what is happening. Once they are more familiar with the play, ask them to hazard a guess as to the exact moment in the play that is depicted.

Navigating the play

Your students may need some help and practice in finding their way around a Shakespeare play. After explaining the division into acts, scenes and lines, challenge them to look up some references as quickly as possible. Refer them to some of the famous lines and those that might lead on to further discussion of the plot. Below are some suggestions:

SCENE 1, LINE 1	ACT 1 (*If music be the food of love, play on*)
SCENE 3, LINE 2	ACT 1 (*I am sure care's an enemy to life*)
SCENE 5, LINES 132–4	ACT 2 (*Some are born great, some achieve greatness, and some have greatness thrust upon 'em*)
SCENE 4, LINES 115–16	ACT 3 (*If this were played upon a stage now, I could condemn it as an improbable fiction*)

Improvisation

Working on one of these improvisations may help students access some of the ideas behind the drama.

a) Ask students to work in threes to create a short improvisation, perhaps based on a current soap opera, in which character A fancies character B, but B fancies C, and C fancies A! How do they behave and react to each other?

b) Ask students to work in small groups. Two of them should take on the part of identical twins. The group should work out a short improvisation in which misunderstandings and chaos arise due to mistaken identities with the twins.

c) Working in small groups, the students should create a scene in a work setting. One of the characters is pompous, bossy and self-important. How do the rest of the characters decide to react towards this character?

Setting the Scene

Comedy

Twelfth Night is a comedy, mainly about romance. The comedic ingredients of the play include twins, unwelcome drunken guests, pompous and love-sick characters. Ask your students what sort of situations they will expect to find in such a play. Not all the romances run smoothly, and there are many misunderstandings. Discuss whether we find the same sort of situations in modern comedies.

The music of love

The opening line of the play is possibly the most famous of Shakespeare's opening lines. It points out the intertwined relationship between love and music. Ask students to consider what the idea refers to and whether music is still the food of love today (e.g. love is featured in pop music, and couples often have a 'special' song). Finally, ask students to consider the different ways in which love is reflected in music.

Illyria

The play is set on an ancient part of the Adriatic coast, which is probably intended as a romantic, faraway, dreamy landscape. Ask students to imagine that they have just arrived on the coast after being shipwrecked. Working in pairs, one should give the other (whose eyes are closed) a guided tour of the coast. The tour could either involve students moving around if you have room, or seated. They should comment on what they can see, hear, and feel in the environment, before swapping roles and continuing the guided tour as they imagine venturing inland.

Keeping Track of the Action

It's important to give students opportunities to 'digest' and reflect upon their reading, so that they may take ownership of the play.

Reading journal

As you read through the play, help students to trace and understand the story by asking them to keep a journal in which they record what happens. They can also record their reactions and thoughts about the action and the characters. Help them to keep their responses focused by giving them specific questions to answer.

Horoscopes

Astrology is mentioned by some of the characters in the play (e.g. Act 1, Scene 3, line 121). Ask students to write horoscopes for different characters at various points in the action. Suitable points in the play are:

- Act 1, Scene 2   Viola – what lies ahead after the shipwreck and loss of her brother?
- Act 1, Scene 5   Olivia – a new person enters her life
- Act 2, Scene 5   Malvolio – all is not as it seems

- Act 4, Scene 1   Sebastian – watch out for newcomers
- Act 5, Scene 1   Orsino – a familiar person has hidden depths.

Ideally, the horoscopes should contain some ambiguity, as well as reflect the students' grasp of the plot and characters.

Storyboarding

In *Bravo, Mr William Shakespeare!*, Marcia Williams (see *Further Reading and Resources* on p. 117) has created colourful and engaging cartoon versions of some of Shakespeare's plays. Cartoon-strip versions of scenes can be helpful for younger students in particular. Give them an example (perhaps through looking at a page of Williams's book) of how to sum up the action, in pictures, captions (explaining what is happening) and speech/thought bubbles (for key words and lines), and then ask them to complete their own storyboard. Suitable scenes might be:

- Act 1, Scene 5   Viola first visits Olivia in the guise of Cesario
- Act 3, Scene 4   Malvolio behaves strangely with Olivia
- Act 3, Scene 4   Viola is challenged to a duel.

Court news

Ask students to write regular bulletins for Orsino's *Court News*. This is a bulletin that tracks the comings and goings at court (e.g. Cesario's arrival) and in the local area (e.g. Sir Andrew's visit), gives up-to-date news on local people of importance (e.g. Olivia), a diary of entertainment and events (e.g. Feste's songs), and gossip about events in the area (e.g. the strange behaviour of Malvolio).

Characters

Students of all ages need to come to an understanding of the characters: their motivations, their relationships, and their development.

Names

Shakespeare often gives clues about the characters in their names. Malvolio, for example, is derived from the Latin 'mal', meaning 'bad', and 'volio' meaning 'I wish'. Sir Toby Belch reminds us of a fat little toby jug and a rather loud burp. Sir Andrew Aguecheek's name derives from 'ague', meaning fever. Ask students to draw cameos of the main characters.

Casting director

Ask your students to cast the parts for a new film or stage version of *Twelfth Night*. First, they will need to construct a profile on the characters, containing information about them (known and surmised). Next, they must make a report on who they are going to invite to take on the parts, and why. Finally, they should give each actor important information about his or her character, and suggestions on how to play the part.

A different perspective

Allowing your students the opportunity to think, write, and talk as one of the characters gives them a new and illuminating perspective on the character(s). Here are some possible tasks:

- Act 1, Scene 3   Sir Andrew creates a video for a dating agency, looking for a partner
- Act 1, Scene 5   Olivia writes a letter to Cesario after their first meeting
- Act 2, Scene 3   Maria writes down her plan to trick Malvolio
- Act 2, Scene 4   Orsino composes a song about what love is like
- Act 5, Scene 1   Antonio explains why he was Orsino's enemy.

Themes

Love

We see different kinds of love, and different attitudes towards love in this play. Ask students to see if they can find evidence of any of the following:

- a man who loves the idea of being in love
- a woman whose love is hidden
- a man who loves himself
- sibling love
- love of friends.

Students could look for other examples of how love is portrayed in the play, and to consider who shows the deepest and most sincere love. Ask for volunteers to take on some of the roles and 'hot seat' them, asking them about their views on love.

Appearances

Outward appearances often fool the main characters in the play. Consider how the following characters are fooled by appearances at different points in the play:

- Olivia
- Orsino
- Sir Andrew
- Malvolio
- Antonio.

Do any of the characters remain clear-sighted throughout the play?

Deception

The play is mostly light-hearted with little malice or real wrong doing. There are deceptions, though, including Viola disguising herself as Cesario and Sir Toby's manipulation of Sir Andrew. The person who seems to come off worst, and who is not reconciled by the end of the play, is Malvolio. Discuss whether the deception involving Malvolio is deserved or 'over the top'.

Shakespeare's Language

Prose and verse

Shakespeare uses prose and verse for different reasons. In this play prose, often the preserve of common characters, is used for the comedy scenes, while verse is used for the more serious and elevated language. Ask students to investigate which characters talk mainly in verse, which in prose, and which characters use both. Challenge them to identify why either verse or prose is used at a particular point.

Imagery

As this play is primarily concerned with love, there are many images that relate to different aspects of love. Love is something to be sought, but it is also the cause of pain and distress. Ask students to look at how the characters describe love, and what they compare it with. For example, look at the speech of the following characters:

- Orsino in Act 1, Scene 1
- Viola in Act 1, Scene 5
- Orsino and Viola in Act 2, Scene 4.

Songs
As well as the verse and prose, the play contains songs which are sung by Feste. These tend to have a sad or reflective tone when discussing love. Ask students to study Feste's style of verse (e.g. the regular rhythm and rhyme), and then to create a poem summing up the events of the play.

Exploring with Drama

Book the hall or push back the desks, because the best way to study a great play is through drama. Students of all ages will benefit from a dramatic encounter with *Twelfth Night*. They will enjoy the opportunity to act out a scene or two, or to explore the situations through improvisation, for example, by putting a character in the 'hot seat' for questioning by others.

Conscience corridor
Viola is in disguise and working for the Duke. Although she has fallen in love with him, she finds herself taking his messages of love to another woman. Ask one student to play the role of Viola, while the rest of the class forms two lines facing each other, making a corridor. One side of the corridor will advise Viola to be honourable and take the messages; the other side of the corridor will urge her to throw aside her disguise and declare her love for him. Viola must walk down the corridor seeking advice. As she passes each student, they will urge her to take their guidance. Once she reaches the end, she must decide what to do.

Tableaux
Ask your students to create a tableau, or freeze-frame, in groups, involving all the main characters in the play. The characters should be grouped together according to their relationships and positions within the play. Bring the tableaux to life briefly, by having each person say something in character.

Comedy acting
Above all else, this play is a comedy. Let students enjoy acting out a comedy scene from the play, for example, Act 3, Scene 4, lines 1–58. Ask students to take on a character from the chosen scene, and appoint one student as the director. The director must then interpret and lead the other students to give an action reading of the scene – they can use their scripts but must act out the lines. Encourage them to use timing, actions, voices and expressions to bring out the comedy of the scene.

Writing about *Twelfth Night*

If your students have to write about *Twelfth Night* for coursework or for examinations, you may wish to give them this general guidance:

- Read the question or task carefully, highlight the key words, and answer all parts of the question.
- Planning is essential. Plan what will be in each paragraph. You can change your plan if necessary.
- Avoid retelling the story.
- *Twelfth Night* is a play – so consider the impact or effect on the audience.
- Use the Point, Evidence, Explanation (PEE) structure to explain points.
- Adding Evaluation (PEEE!) will gain you higher marks.
- Keep quotations short and relevant.
- Avoid referring to a film version of the play, unless this is part of your task.

The Shakespeare Birthplace Trust
Information on his works, life and times.
http://www.shakespeare.org.uk/homepage

Shakespeare's Globe
Information on The Globe Theatre, London.
http://www.shakespeares-globe.org/

Shakespeare Illustrated
An excellent source of paintings and pictures based on Shakespeare's plays.
http://www.emory.edu/ENGLISH/classes/Shakespeare_Illustrated/
Shakespeare.html

Spark Notes: Twelfth Night
An online study guide.
http://www.sparknotes.com/shakespeare/twelfthnight/

Twelfth Night Revision Site
Notes and games on the play.
http://www.twelfthnightsite.co.uk/index.htm

Mr William Shakespeare and the Internet
A comprehensive guide to Shakespeare resources on the Internet.
http://shakespeare.palomar.edu/

Film, video, DVD and Audio
Twelfth Night
BBC TV Shakespeare Collection (1980)

Twelfth Night
Directed by Kenneth Brannagh, starring Richard Briers (1988)

The Animated Tales of Shakespeare
Part of a boxed set of 12 plays (1992)

Twelfth Night
Directed by Trevor Nunn, starring Helena Bonham Carter (1996)

Twelfth Night
New Cambridge Shakespeare Audio (audio cassette) (1999)

Twelfth Night
Naxos audio books (audio CD) (1999)

Further Reading and Resources

General
Fantasia, Louis, *Instant Shakespeare: A Practical Guide for Actors, Directors and Teachers* (A & C Black, 2002).
Greer, Germaine, *Shakespeare: A Very Short Introduction* (Oxford, 2002).
Hall, Peter, *Shakespeare's Advice to the Players* (Oberon Books, 2003).
Holden, Anthony, *Shakespeare: His Life and Work* (Abacus, 2002).
Kneen, Judith, *Teaching Shakespeare from Transition to Test* (Oxford University Press, 2004).
McConnell, Louise, *Exit, Pursued by a Bear – Shakespeare's Characters, Plays, Poems, History and Stagecraft* (Bloomsbury, 2003).
McLeish, Kenneth, and Unwin, Stephen, *A Pocket Guide to Shakespeare's Plays*, (Faber and Faber, 1998).
Muirden, James, *Shakespeare in a Nutshell: A Rhyming Guide to All the Plays* (Constable, 2004).
Wood, Michael, *In Search of Shakespeare* (BBC, 2003).

Children's/Students' Books
Carpenter, Humphrey, *More Shakespeare Without the Boring Bits* (Viking, 1997).
Deary, Terry, *Top Ten Shakespeare Stories* (Scholastic, 1998).
Ganeri, Anita, *What They Don't Tell You About Shakespeare* (Hodder, 1996).
Garfield, Leon, *Shakespeare Stories* (Puffin, 1997).
Garfield, Leon, *Shakespeare: The Animated Tales* (Egmont, 2002).
Lamb, Charles and Mary, *Tales from Shakespeare* (Puffin edition, 1987).
McCaughrean, Geraldine, *Stories from Shakespeare* (Orion, 1997).
Williams, Marcia, *Bravo, Mr William Shakespeare!* (Walker, 2001).

Websites
The Complete Works of Shakespeare
http://the-tech.mit.edu/Shakespeare/

Elizabethan pronunciation
Including information on insults.
http://www.renfaire.com/Language/index.html

Encyclopaedia Britannica – Shakespeare and the Globe: Then and Now
Information about the Globe and the theatre in Shakespeare's times.
http://search.eb.com/shakespeare/index2.html

The Royal Shakespeare Company website
As well as information on the theatre company, this contains resources on the plays and the life and times of Shakespeare.
http://www.rsc.org.uk/home/default.aspx